Do And Dare - A Brave Boy's Fight For Fortune

By
Horatio Alger

CHAPTER I. THE POST OFFICE AT WAYNEBORO.

"If we could only keep the post office, mother, we should be all right," said Herbert Carr, as he and his mother sat together in the little sitting room of the plain cottage which the two had occupied ever since he was a boy of five.

"Yes, Herbert, but I am afraid there won't be much chance of it."

"Who would want to take it from you, mother?"

"Men are selfish, Herbert, and there is no office, however small, that is not sought after."

"What was the income last year?" inquired Herbert.

Mrs. Carr referred to a blank book lying on the table in which the post-office accounts were kept, and answered:

"Three hundred and ninety-eight dollars and fifty cents."

"I shouldn't think that would be much of an inducement to an able-bodied man, who could work at any business."

"Your father was glad to have it."

"Yes, mother, but he had lost an arm in the war, and could not engage in any business that required both hands."

"That is true, Herbert, but I am afraid there will be more than one who will be willing to relieve me of the duties. Old Mrs. Allen called at the office to-day, and told me she understood that there was a movement on foot to have Ebenezer Graham appointed."

"Squire Walsingham's nephew?"

"Yes; it is understood that the squire will throw his influence into the scale, and that will probably decide the matter."

"Then it's very mean of Squire Walsingham," said Herbert, indignantly. "He knows that you depend on the office for a living."

"Most men are selfish, my dear Herbert."

"But he was an old schoolfellow of father's, and it was as his substitute that father went to the war where he was wounded."

"True, Herbert, but I am afraid that consideration won't weigh much with John Walsingham."

"I have a great mind to go and see him, mother. Have you any objections?"

"I have no objections, but I am afraid it will do no good."

"Mr. Graham ought to be ashamed, with the profits of his store, to want the post office also. His store alone pays him handsomely."

"Mr. Graham is fond of money. He means to be a rich man."

"That is true enough. He is about the meanest man in town."

A few words are needed in explanation, though the conversation explains itself pretty well.

Herbert's father, returning from the war with the loss of an arm, was fortunate enough to receive the appointment of postmaster, and thus earn a small, but, with strict economy, adequate income, until a fever terminated his earthly career at middle age. Mr. Graham was a rival applicant for the office, but Mr. Carr's services in the war were thought to give him superior claims, and he secured it. During the month that had elapsed since his death, Mrs. Carr had carried on the post office under a temporary appointment. She was a woman of good business capacity, and already familiar with the duties of the office, having assisted her husband, especially during his sickness, when nearly the whole work devolved upon her. Most of the village people were in favor of having her retained, but the local influence of Squire Walsingham and his nephew was so great that a petition in favor of the latter secured numerous signatures, and was already on file at the department in Washington, and backed by the congressman of the district, who was a political friend of the squire. Mrs. Carr was not aware that the movement for her displacement had gone so far.

It was already nine o'clock when Herbert's conversation with his mother ended, and he resolved to defer his call upon Squire Walsingham till the next morning.

About nine o'clock in the forenoon our young hero rang the bell of the village magnate, and with but little delay was ushered into his presence.

Squire Walsingham was a tall, portly man of fifty, sleek and evidently on excellent terms with himself. Indeed, he was but five years older than his nephew, Ebenezer Graham, and looked the younger of the two, despite the relationship. If he had been a United States Senator he could not have been more dignified in his deportment, or esteemed himself of greater consequence. He was a selfish man, but he was free from the mean traits that characterized his nephew.

"You are the Carr boy," said the squire, pompously, looking over his spectacles at Herbert, as he entered the door.

"My name is Herbert Carr," said Herbert, shortly. "You have known me all my life."

"Certainly," said the squire, a little ruffled at the failure of his grand manner to impose upon his young visitor. "Did I not call you the Carr boy?"

Herbert did not fancy being called the Carr boy, but he was there to ask a favor, and he thought it prudent not to show his dissatisfaction. He resolved to come to the point at once.

"I have called, Squire Walsingham," he commenced, "to ask if you will use your influence to have my mother retained in charge of the post office."

"Ahem!" said the squire, somewhat embarrassed. "I am not in charge of the post-office department."

"No, sir, I am aware of that; but the postmaster general will be influenced by the recommendations of people in the village."

"Very true!" said the squire, complacently. "Very true, and very proper. I do not pretend to say that my recommendation would not weigh with the authorities at Washington. Indeed, the member from our district is a personal friend of mine."

"You know how we are situated," continued Herbert, who thought it best to state his case as briefly as possible. "Father was unable to save anything, and we have no money ahead. If mother can keep the post office, we shall get along nicely, but if she loses it, we shall have a hard time."

"I am surprised that in your father's long tenure of office he did not save something," said the squire, in a tone which indicated not only surprise but reproof.

"There was not much chance to save on a salary of four hundred dollars a year," said Herbert, soberly, "after supporting a family of three."

"Ahem!" said the squire, sagely; "where there's a will there's a way. Improvidence is the great fault of the lower classes."

"We don't belong to the lower classes," said Herbert, flushing with indignation.

Squire Walmsgham was secretly ambitious of representing his district some day in Congress, and he felt that he had made a mistake. It won't do for an aspirant to office to speak of the lower classes, and the squire hastened to repair his error.

"That was not the term I intended to imply," he condescended to explain. "I meant to say that improvidence is the prevailing fault of those whose income is small."

"We haven't had much chance to be improvident!" said Herbert "We have had to spend all our income, but we are not in debt—that is, we have no debts that we are unable to pay."

"That is well," said Squire Walsingham, "but, my young constituent—I mean my young friend—I apprehend that you do not take a right view of public office. It is not designed to support a privileged class in luxury."

"Luxury, on four hundred a year!" replied Herbert.

"I am speaking in general terms," said the squire, hastily. "I mean to say that I cannot recommend a person to office simply because he or she needs the income."

"No, sir, I know that; but my mother understands the duties of the office, and no complaint has been made that she does not make a good postmaster."

"Possibly," said the squire, non-commitally; "but I am opposed upon principle to conferring offices upon women. Men are more efficient, and better qualified to discharge responsible duties."

"Then, sir," said Herbert, his heart sinking, "I am to understand that you do not favor the appointment of my mother?"

"I should be glad to hear that your mother was doing well," said the squire, "but I cannot conscientiously favor the appointment of a woman to be postmaster of Wayneboro."

"That means that he prefers the appointment should go to his nephew," thought Herbert.

"If my mother were not competent to discharge the duties," he said, his face showing his disappointment in spite of himself, "I would not ask your influence, notwithstanding you were a schoolmate of father's, and he lost his arm while acting as your substitute."

"I have already said that I wish your mother well," said the squire, coloring, "and in any other way I am ready to help her and you. Indeed, I may be able to secure you a situation."

"Where, sir?"

"Mr. Graham needs a boy in his store, and I think he will take you on my recommendation."

"Is Tom Tripp going away?" asked Herbert.

"The Tripp boy is unsatisfactory, so Mr. Graham tells me."

Herbert knew something of what it would be to be employed by Mr. Graham. Tom Tripp worked early and late for a dollar and a half per week, without board, for a hard and suspicious taskmaster, who was continually finding fault with him. But for sheer necessity, he would have left Mr. Graham's store long ago. He had confided the unpleasantness of his position to Herbert more than once, and enlisted his sympathy and indignation. Herbert felt that he would not like to work for Mr. Graham at any price, more especially as it seemed likely that the storekeeper was likely to deprive his mother of her office and income.

"I should not like to work for Mr. Graham, sir," he said.

"It appears to me that you are very particular, young man," said Squire Walsingham.

"I would be willing to work for you, sir, but not for him."

"Ahem!" said the squire, somewhat mollified, "I will think of your case."

Herbert left the house, feeling that his mother's removal was only a matter of time.

CHAPTER II. HERBERT'S CHANCE.

Herbert left the house of Squire Walsingham in a sober frame of mind. He saw clearly that his mother would not long remain in office, and without her official income they would find it hard to get along. To be sure, she received a pension of eight dollars a month, in consideration of her husband's services in the war, but eight dollars would not go far towards supporting their family, small as it was. There were other means of earning a living, to be sure, but Wayneboro was an agricultural town mainly, and unless he hired out on a farm there seemed no way open to him, while the little sewing his mother might be able to procure would probably pay her less than a dollar a week.

The blow fell sooner than he expected. In the course of the next week Mrs. Carr was notified that Ebenezer Graham had been appointed her successor, and she was directed to turn over the papers and property of the office to him.

She received the official notification by the afternoon mail, and in the evening she was favored by a call from her successor.

Ebenezer Graham was a small man, with insignificant, mean-looking features, including a pair of weazel-like eyes and a turn-up nose. It did not require a skillful physiognomist to read his character in his face. Meanness was stamped upon it in unmistakable characters.

"Good-evening, Mr. Graham," said the widow, gravely.

"Good-evening, ma'am," said the storekeeper. "I've called to see you, Mrs. Carr, about the post office, I presume you have heard—"

"I have heard that you are to be my successor."

"Just so. As long as your husband was alive, I didn't want to step into his shoes."

"But you are willing to step into mine," said Mrs. Carr, smiling faintly.

"Just so—that is, the gov'ment appear to think a man ought to be in charge of so responsible a position."

"I shall be glad if you manage the office better than I have done."

"You see, ma'am, it stands to reason that a man is better fitted for business than a woman," said Ebenezer Graham, in a smooth tone for he wanted to get over this rather awkward business as easily as possible. "Women, you know, was made to adorn the domestic circles, et cetery."

"Adorning the domestic circle won't give me a living," said Mrs. Carr, with some bitterness, for she knew that but for the grasping spirit of the man before her she would have been allowed to retain her office.

"I was comin' to that," said the new postmaster. "Of course, I appreciate your position as a widder, without much means, and I'm going to make you an offer; that is, your boy, Herbert."

Herbert looked up from a book he was reading, and listened with interest to hear the benevolent intentions of the new postmaster.

"I am ready to give him a place in my store," proceeded Ebenezer. "I always keep a boy, and thinks I to myself, the wages I give will help along the widder Carr. You see, I like to combine business with consideration for my feller creeters."

Mrs. Carr smiled faintly, for in spite of her serious strait she could not help being amused at the notion of Ebenezer Graham's philanthropy.

"What's going to become of Tom Tripp?" asked Herbert, abruptly.

"Thomas Tripp isn't exactly the kind of boy I want in my store," said Mr. Graham. "He's a harum-scarum sort of boy, and likes to shirk his work. Then I suspect he stops to play on the way when I send him on errands. Yesterday he was five minutes longer than he need to have been in goin' to Sam Dunning's to carry some groceries. Thomas doesn't seem to appreciate his privileges in bein' connected with a business like mine."

Tom Tripp was hardly to blame for not recognizing his good luck in occupying a position where he received a dollar and a half a week for fourteen hours daily work, with half a dozen scoldings thrown in.

"How do you know I will suit you any better than Tom?" asked Herbert, who did not think it necessary to thank Mr. Graham for the proffered engagement until he learned just what was expected of him, and what his pay was to be.

"You're a different sort of a boy," said Ebenezer, with an attempt at a pleasant smile. "You've been brought up different. I've heard you're a smart, capable boy, that isn't afraid of work."

"No, sir, I am not, if I am fairly paid for my work."

The new postmaster's jaw fell, and he looked uneasy, for he always grudged the money he paid out, even the paltry dollar and a half which went to poor Tom.

"I always calkerlate to pay fair wages," he said; "but I ain't rich, and I can't afford to fling away money."

"How much do you pay Tom Tripp?" asked Herbert.

He knew, but he wanted to draw Mr. Graham out.

"I pay Thomas a dollar and fifty cents a week," answered the storekeeper, in a tone which indicated that he regarded this, on the whole, as rather a munificent sum.

"And he works from seven in the morning till nine o'clock at night," proceeded Herbert.

"Them are the hours," said Ebenezer, who knew better how to make money than to speak grammatically.

"It makes a pretty long day," observed Mrs. Carr.

"So it does, ma'am, but it's no longer than I work myself."

"You get paid rather better, I presume."

"Of course, ma'am, as I am the proprietor."

"I couldn't think of working for any such sum," said Herbert, decidedly.

Mr. Graham looked disturbed, for he had reasons for desiring to secure Herbert, who was familiar with the routine of post-office work.

"Well," he said, "I might be able to offer you a leetle more, as you know how to tend the post office. That's worth somethin'! I'll give you—lemme see—twenty-five cents more; that is, a dollar and seventy-five cents a week."

Herbert and his mother exchanged glances. They hardly knew whether to feel more amused or disgusted at their visitor's meanness.

"Mr. Graham," said Herbert, "if you wish to secure my services, you will have to pay me three dollars a week."

The storekeeper held up both hands in dismay.

"Three dollars a week for a boy!" he exclaimed.

"Yes, sir; I will come for a short time for that sum, till you get used to the management of the post office, but I shall feel justified in leaving you when I can do better."

"You must think I am made of money," said Ebenezer hastily.

"I think you can afford to pay me that salary."

For twenty minutes the new postmaster tried to beat down his prospective clerk, but Herbert was obstinate, and Ebenezer rather ruefully promised to give him his price, chiefly because it was absolutely necessary that he should engage some one who was more familiar with the post-office work than he was. Herbert agreed to go to work the next morning.

CHAPTER III. A PRODIGAL SON.

Herbert did not look forward with very joyful anticipations to the new engagement he had formed. He knew very well that he should not like Ebenezer Graham as an employer, but it was necessary that he should earn something, for the income was now but two dollars a week. He was sorry, too, to displace Tom Tripp, but upon this point his uneasiness was soon removed, for Tom dropped in just after Mr. Graham had left the house, and informed Herbert that he was to go to work the next day for a farmer in the neighborhood, at a dollar and a half per week, and board besides.

"I am glad to hear it, Tom," said Herbert, heartily. "I didn't want to feel that I was depriving you of employment."

"You are welcome to my place in the store," said Tom. "I'm glad to give it up. Mr. Graham seemed to think I was made of iron, and I could work like a machine, without getting tired. I hope he pays you more than a dollar and a half a week."

"He has agreed to pay me three dollars," said Herbert.

Tom whistled in genuine amazement.

"What! has the old man lost his senses?" he exclaimed. "He must be crazy to offer such wages as that."

"He didn't offer them. I told him I wouldn't come for less."

"I don't see how he came to pay such a price."

"Because he wanted me to take care of the post office. I know all about it, and he doesn't."

"As soon as he learns, he will reduce your wages."

"Then I shall leave him."

"Well, I hope you'll like store work better than I do."

The next two or three days were spent in removing the post office to one corner of Eben-ezer Graham's store. The removal was superintended by Herbert, who was not interfered with to any extent by his employer, nor required to do much work in the store. Our hero was agreeably surprised, and began to think he should get along better than he anticipated.

At the end of the first week the storekeeper, while they were closing the shutters, said: "I expect, Herbert, you'd just as lieves take your pay in groceries and goods from the store?"

"No, sir," answered Herbert, "I prefer to be paid in money, and to pay for such goods as we buy."

"I don't see what odds it makes to you," said Ebenezer. "It comes to the same thing, doesn't it?"

"Then if it comes to the same thing," retorted Herbert, "why do you want to pay me in goods?"

"Ahem! It saves trouble. I'll just charge everything you buy, and give you the balance Saturday night."

"I should prefer the money, Mr. Graham," said Herbert, firmly.

So the storekeeper, considerably against his will, drew three dollars in bills from the drawer and handed them to his young clerk.

"It's a good deal of money, Herbert," he said, "for a boy. There ain't many men would pay you such a good salary."

"I earn every cent of it, Mr. Graham," said Herbert, whose views on the salary question differed essentially from those of his employer.

The next morning Mr. Graham received a letter which evidently disturbed him. Before referring to its contents, it is necessary to explain that he had one son, nineteen years of age, who had gone to Boston two years previous, to take a place in a dry-goods store on Washington Street. Ebenezer Graham, Jr., or Eben, as he was generally called, was, in some respects, like his father. He had the same features, and was quite as mean, so far as others were concerned, but willing to spend money for his own selfish pleasures. He was fond of playing pool, and cards, and had contracted a dangerous fondness for whisky, which consumed all the money he could spare from necessary expenses, and even more, so that, as will presently appear, he failed to meet his board bills regularly. Eben had served an apprenticeship in his father's store, having been, in fact, Tom Tripp's predecessor; he tired of his father's strict discipline, and the small pay out of which he was required to purchase his clothes, and went to Boston to seek a wider sphere.

To do Eben justice, it must be admitted that he had good business capacity, and if he had been able, like his father, to exercise self-denial, and make money-getting his chief enjoyment, he would no doubt have become a rich man in time. As it was, whenever he could make his companions pay for his pleasures, he did so.

I now come to the letter which had brought disquietude to the storekeeper.

It ran thus:

"DEAR SIR: I understand that you are the father of Mr. Eben Graham, who has been a boarder at my house for the last six months. I regret to trouble you, but he is now owing me six weeks board, and I cannot get a cent out of him, though he knows I am a poor widow, dependent on my board money for my rent and house expenses. As he is a minor, the law makes you responsible for his bills, and, though I dislike to trouble you, I am obliged, in justice to myself, to ask you to settle his board bill, which I inclose.

"You will do me a great favor if you will send me the amount—thirty dollars—within a week, as my rent is coming due.

"Yours respectfully, SUSAN JONES."

The feelings of a man like Ebenezer Graham can be imagined when he read this unpleasant missive.

"Thirty dollars!" he groaned. "What can the graceless boy be thinking of, to fool away his money, and leave his bills to be settled by me. If this keeps on, I shall be ruined! It's too bad, when I am slaving here, for Eben to waste my substance on riotous living. I've a great mind to disown him. Let him go his own way, and fetch up in the poorhouse, if he chooses."

But it is not easy for a man to cast off an only son, even though he is as poorly supplied with natural affections as Ebenezer Graham. Besides, Eben's mother interceded for him, and the father, in bitterness of spirit, was about to mail a registered letter to Mrs. Jones, when the cause of his anguish suddenly made his appearance in the store.

"How are you, father?" he said, nonchalantly, taking a cigar from his mouth. "Didn't expect to see me, did you?"

"What brings you here, Eben?" asked Mr. Graham, uneasily.

"Well, the cars brought me to Stockton, and I've walked the rest of the way."

"I've heard of you," said his father, frowning. "I got a letter last night from Mrs. Jones."

"She said she was going to write," said Eben, shrugging his shoulders.

"How came it," said his father, his voice trembling with anger, "that you haven't paid your board bill for six weeks?"

"I didn't have the money," said Eben, with a composure which was positively aggravating to his father.

"And why didn't you have the money? Your wages are ample to pay all your expenses."

"It costs more money to live in Boston than you think for, father."

"Don't you get ten dollars a week, sir? At your age I got only seven, and saved two dollars a week."

"You didn't live in Boston, father."

"I didn't smoke cigars," said his father, angrily, as he fixed his eye on the one his son was smoking. "How much did you pay for that miserable weed?"

"You're mistaken, father. It's a very good article. I paid eight dollars a hundred."

"Eight dollars a hundred!" gasped Mr. Graham. "No wonder you can't pay your board bill—I can't afford to spend my money on cigars."

"Oh, yes, you can, father, if you choose. Why, you're a rich man."

"A rich man!" repeated Mr. Graham, nervously. "It would take a rich man to pay your bills. But you haven't told me why you have come home."

"I lost my situation, father—some meddlesome fellow told my employer that I occasionally played a game of pool, and my tailor came to the store and dunned me; so old Boggs gave me a long lecture and my walking papers, and here I am."

Ebenezer Graham was sorely troubled, and, though he isn't a favorite of mine, I confess, that in this matter he has my sincere sympathy.

CHAPTER IV. HERBERT LOSES HIS PLACE.

Ebenezer Graham with some difficulty ascertained from Eben that he had other bills, amounting in the aggregate to forty-seven dollars. This added to the board bill, made a total of seventy-seven dollars. Mr. Graham's face elongated perceptibly.

"That is bad enough," he said; "but you have lost your income also, and that makes matters worse. Isn't there a chance of the firm taking you back?"

"No, sir," replied the prodigal. "You see, we had a flare up, and I expressed my opinion of them pretty plainly. They wouldn't take me back if I'd come for nothing."

"And they won't give you a recommendation, either?" said Ebenezer, with a half groan.

"No, sir; I should say not."

"So you have ruined your prospects so far as Boston is concerned," said his father, bitterly. "May I ask how you expect to get along?"

"I have a plan," said Eben, with cheerful confidence.

"What is it?"

"I would like to go to California. If I can't get any situation in San Francisco, I can go to the mines."

"Very fine, upon my word!" said his father, sarcastically. "And how do you propose to get to California?"

"I can go either by steamer, across the isthmus, or over the Union Pacific road."

"That isn't what I mean. Where are you to get the money to pay your fare with?"

"I suppose you will supply that," said Eben.

"You do? Well, it strikes me you have some assurance," ejaculated Mr. Graham. "You expect me to advance hundreds of dollars, made by working early and late, to support a spendthrift son!"

"I'll pay you back as soon as I am able," said Eben, a little abashed.

"No doubt! You'd pay me in the same way you pay your board bills," said Ebenezer, who may be excused for the sneer. "I can invest my money to better advantage than upon you."

"Then, if you will not do that," said Eben, sullenly, "I will leave you to suggest a plan."

"There is only one plan I can think of, Eben. Go back to your old place in the store. I will dismiss the Carr boy, and you can attend to the post office, and do the store work."

"What, go back to tending a country grocery, after being a salesman in a city store!" exclaimed Eben, disdainfully.

"Yes, it seems the only thing you have left. It's your own fault that you are not still a salesman in the city."

Eben took the cigar from his mouth, and thought rapidly.

"Well," he said, after a pause, "if I agree to do this, what will you pay me?"

"What will I pay you?"

"Yes, will you pay me ten dollars a week—the same as I got at Hanbury & Deane's?"

"Ten dollars a week!" ejaculated Ebenezer, "I don't get any more than that myself."

"I guess there's a little mistake in your calculations, father," said Eben, significantly. "If you don't make at least forty dollars a week, including the post office, then I am mistaken."

"So you are—ridiculously mistaken!" said his father, sharply. "What you presume is entirely out of the question. You forget that you will be getting your board, and Tom Tripp only received a dollar and a half a week without board."

"Is that all you pay to Herbert Carr?"

"I pay him a leetle more," admitted Ebenezer.

"What will you give me?"

"I'll give you your board and clothes," said Ebenezer, "and that seems to be more than you made in Boston."

"Are you in earnest?" asked Eben, in genuine dismay.

"Certainly. It isn't a bad offer, either."

"Do you suppose a young man like me can get along without money?"

"You ought to get along without money for the next two years, after the sums you've wasted in Boston. It will cripple me to pay your bills," and the storekeeper groaned at the thought of the inroads the payment would make on his bank account.

"You're poorer than I thought, if seventy-five dollars will cripple you," said Eben, who knew his father's circumstances too well to be moved by this representation.

"I shall be in the poorhouse before many years if I undertake to pay all your bills, Eben."

After all, this was not, perhaps, an exaggeration, for a spendthrift son can get through a great deal of money.

"I can't get along without money, father," said Eben, decidedly. "How can I buy cigars, let alone other things?"

"I don't want you to smoke cigars. You'll be a great deal better off without them," said his father, sharply.

"I understand; it's necessary to my health," said Eben, rather absurdly.

"You won't smoke at my expense," said Ebenezer, decidedly. "I don't smoke myself, and I never knew any good come of it."

"All the same, I must have some money. What will people say about a young man of my age not having a cent in his pocket? They think my father is very mean."

"I'll allow you fifty cents a week," said Mr. Graham, after a pause.

"That won't do! You seem to think I am only six or seven years old!"

Finally, after considerable haggling, Mr. Graham agreed to pay his son a dollar and a half a week, in cash, besides board and clothes. He reflected that he should be obliged to board and clothe his son at any rate, and should save a dollar and a half from Herbert's wages.

"Well," he said, "when will you be ready to go to work?"

"I must have a few days to loaf, father. I have been hard at work for a long time, and need some rest."

"Then you can begin next Monday morning. I'll get Herbert to show you how to prepare the mail, so that you won't have any trouble about the post-office work."

"By the way, father, how do you happen to have the post office? I thought Mrs. Carr was to carry it on."

"So she did, for a time, but a woman ain't fit for a public position of that kind. So I applied for the position, and got it."

"What's Mrs. Carr going to do?"

"She's got her pension," said Ebenezer, shortly.

"Eight dollars a month, isn't it?"

"Yes."

"That ain't much to support a family."

"She'll have to do something else, then, I suppose."

"There isn't much to do in Wayneboro."

"That isn't my lookout. She can take in sewing, or washing," suggested Ebenezer, who did not trouble himself much about the care of his neighbors. "Besides there's Herbert—he can earn something."

"But I'm to take his place."

"Oh well, I ain't under any obligations to provide them a livin'. I've got enough to take care of myself and my family."

"You'd better have let her keep the post office," said Eben. He was not less selfish than his father, but then his own interests were not concerned. He would not have scrupled, in his father's case, to do precisely the same.

"It's lucky I've got a little extra income," said Ebenezer, bitterly; "now I've got your bills to pay."

"I suppose I shall have to accept your offer, father," said Eben, "for the present; but I hope you'll think better of my California plan after a while. Why, there's a fellow I know went out there last year, went up to the mines, and now he's worth five thousand dollars!"

"Then he must be a very different sort of a person from you," retorted his father, sagaciously. "You would never succeed there, if you can't in Boston."

"I've never had a chance to try," grumbled Eben.

There was sound sense in what his father said. Failure at home is very likely to be followed by failure away from home. There have been cases that seemed to disprove my assertion, but in such cases failure has only been changed into success by earnest work. I say to my young readers, therefore, never give up a certainty at home to tempt the chances of success in a distant State, unless you are prepared for disappointment.

When the engagement had been made with Eben, Mr. Graham called Herbert to his presence.

"Herbert," said he, "I won't need you after Saturday night. My son is going into the store, and will do all I require. You can tell him how to prepare the mails, et cetery."

"Very well, sir," answered Herbert. It was not wholly a surprise, but it was a disappointment, for he did not know how he could make three dollars a week in any other way, unless he left Wayneboro.

CHAPTER V. EBEN'S SCHEME.

Saturday night came, and with it the end of Herbert's engagement in the post office.

He pocketed the three dollars which his employer grudgingly gave him, and set out on his way home.

"Wait a minute, Herbert," said Eben. "I'll walk with you."

Herbert didn't care much for Eben's company but he was too polite to say so. He waited therefore, till Eben appeared with hat and cane.

"I'm sorry to cut you out of your place, Herbert," said the young man.

"Thank you," answered Herbert.

"It isn't my fault, for I don't want to go into the store," proceeded Eben. "A fellow that's stood behind the counter in a city store is fit for something better, but it's the old man's fault."

Herbert made no comment, and Eben proceeded:

"Yes," said he, "it's the old man's fault. He's awfully stingy, you know that yourself."

Herbert did know it, but thought it would not be in good taste to say so.

"I suppose Wayneboro is rather dull for you after living in the city," he remarked.

"I should say so. This village is a dull hole, and yet father expects me to stay here cooped up in a little country store. I won't stay here long, you may be sure of that."

"Where will you go?"

"I don't know yet. I want to go to California, but I can't unless the old man comes down with the requisite amount of tin. You'll soon have your situation back again. I won't stand in your way."

"I'm not very particular about going back," said Herbert, "but I must find something to do."

"Just so!" said Eben. "The place will do well enough for a boy like you, but I am a young man, and entitled to look higher. By the way, I've got something in view that may bring me in five thousand dollars within a month."

Herbert stared at his companion in surprise, not knowing any short cut to wealth.

"Do you mean it?" he asked, incredulously.

"Yes," said Eben.

"I suppose you don't care to tell what it is?"

"Oh, I don't mind—it's a lottery."

"Oh!" said Herbert, in a tone of disappointment.

"Yes," answered Eben. "You may think lotteries are a fraud and all that, but I know a man in Boston who drew last month a prize of fifteen thousand dollars. The ticket only cost him a dollar. What do you say to that?"

"Such cases can't be very common," said Herbert, who had a good share of common sense.

"Not so uncommon as you think," returned Eben, nodding. "I don't mean to say that many draw prizes as large as that, but there are other prizes of five thousand dollars, and one thousand, and so on. It would be very comfortable to draw a prize of even five hundred, wouldn't it now?"

Herbert admitted that it would.

"I'd send for a ticket by Monday morning's mail," continued Eben, "if I wasn't so hard up. The old man's mad because I ran into debt, and he won't give me a cent. Will you do me a favor?"

"What is it?" asked Herbert, cautiously.

"Lend me two dollars. You've got it, I know, because you were paid off to-night. I would send for two tickets, and agree to give you quarter of what I draw. Isn't that fair?"

"It may be," said Herbert, "but I haven't any money to lend."

"You have three dollars in your pocket at this moment."

"Yes, but it isn't mine. I must hand it to mother."

"And give up the chance of winning a prize. I'll promise to give you half of whatever I draw, besides paying back the money."

"Thank you, but I can't spare the money."

"You are getting as miserly as the old man," said Eben, with a forced laugh.

"Eben," said Herbert, seriously, "you don't seem to understand our position. Mother has lost the post office, and has but eight dollars a month income. I've earned three dollars this week, but next week I may earn nothing. You see, I can't afford to spend money for lottery tickets."

"Suppose by your caution you lose five hundred dollars. Nothing risk, nothing gain!"

"I have no money to risk," said Herbert, firmly.

"Oh, well, do as you please!" said Eben, evidently disappointed. "I thought I'd make you the offer, because I should like to see you win a big prize."

"Thank you for your friendly intention," said Herbert, "but I am afraid there are a good many more blanks than prizes. If there were not, it wouldn't pay the lottery men to carry on the business."

This was common sense, and I cannot forbear at this point to press it upon the attention of my young reader. Of all schemes of gaining wealth, about the most foolish is spending money for lottery tickets. It has been estimated by a sagacious writer that there is about as much likelihood of drawing a large prize in a lottery as of being struck by lightning and that, let us hope, is very small.

"I guess I won't go any farther," said Eben, abruptly, having become convinced that Herbert could not be prevailed upon to lend him money.

"Good-night, then," said Herbert "Good-night."

"Well, mother, I'm out of work," said Herbert, as he entered the little sitting room, and threw down his week's wages. Our young hero was of a cheerful temperament but he looked and felt sober when he said this.

"But for the Grahams we should have a comfortable living," the boy proceeded. "First, the father took away the post office from you, and now the son has robbed me of my place."

"Don't be discouraged, Herbert," said his mother. "God will find us a way out of our troubles."

Herbert had been trained to have a reverence for religion, and had faith in the providential care of his heavenly Father, and his mother's words recalled his cheerfulness.

"You are right, mother," he said, more hopefully. "I was feeling low-spirited to-night, but I won't feel so any more. I don't see how we are to live, but I won't let it trouble me tonight."

"Let us do our part, and leave the rest to God," said Mrs. Carr. "He won't support us in idleness, but I am sure that in some way relief will come if we are ready to help ourselves."

"God helps them that help themselves," repeated Herbert.

"Exactly so. To-morrow is Sunday, and we won't let any worldly anxieties spoil that day for us. When Monday comes, we will think over what is best to be done."

The next day Herbert and his mother attended church in neat apparel, and those who saw their cheerful faces were not likely to guess the serious condition of their affairs. They were not in debt, to be sure, but, unless employment came soon, they were likely to be ere long, for they had barely enough money ahead to last them two weeks.

Monday morning came, and brought its burden of care.

"I wish there was a factory in Wayneboro," said Herbert. "I am told that boys of my age sometimes earn six or seven dollars a week."

"I have heard so. Here there seems nothing, except working on a farm."

"And the farmers expect boys to take their pay principally in board."

"That is a consideration, but, if possible, I hope we shall not be separated at meals."

"I will try other things first," said Herbert. "How would you like some fish for dinner, mother? My time isn't of any particular value, and I might as well go fishing."

"Do so, Herbert. It will save our buying meat, which, indeed, we can hardly afford to do."

Herbert felt that anything was better than idleness, so he took his pole from the shed, and, after digging a supply of bait, set out for the banks of the river half a mile away.

Through a grassy lane leading from the main street, he walked down to the river with the pole on his shoulder.

He was not destined to solitude, for under a tree whose branches hung over the river sat a young man, perhaps twenty-five years of age, with a book in his hand.

CHAPTER VI. HERBERT'S GOOD LUCK.

"Good-morning," said the young man, pleasantly.

"Good-morning," answered Herbert, politely.

He recognized the young man, though he had never seen him before, as a visitor from the city, who was boarding at the hotel, if the village tavern could be so designated. He seemed to be a studious young man, for he always had a book in his hand. He had a pleasant face, but was pale and slender, and was evidently in poor health.

"I see you are going to try your luck at fishing," said the young man.

"Yes, sir; I have nothing else to do, and that brings me here."

"I, too, have nothing else to do; but I judge from your appearance that you have not the same reason for being idle."

"What is that, sir?"

"Poor health."

"No, sir; I have never been troubled in that way."

"You are fortunate. Health is a blessing not to be overestimated. It is better than money."

"I suppose it is, sir; but at present I think I should value a little money."

"Are you in want of it?" asked the young man, earnestly.

"Yes, sir; I have just lost my place in the post office."

"I think I have seen you in the post office."

"Yes, sir; my mother had charge of the office till two weeks since, when it was transferred to Mr. Graham. He employed me to attend to the duties, and serve the customers in the store, till Saturday night, when I was succeeded by his son, who had just returned from the city."

"Your mother is a widow, is she not?"

"Yes, sir."

"I know where you live; I have had it pointed out to me. Your father served in the war, did he not?"

"Yes, sir; and the injuries he received hastened his death."

The young man looked thoughtful. Then he said: "How much did Mr. Graham pay you for your services?"

"Three dollars a week."

"That was not—excuse the question—all you and your mother had to depend upon, was it?"

"Not quite; mother receives a pension of eight dollars per month."

"Five dollars a week altogether—that is very little."

"It is only two dollars now, sir."

"True; but you have health and strength, and those will bring money. In one respect you are more fortunate than I. You have a mother—I have neither father nor mother."

"I'm sorry for you, sir."

"Thank you; anyone is to be pitied who has lost his parents. Now, as I have asked about your affairs, it is only fair that I should tell you about myself. To begin with, I am rich. Don't look envious, for there is something to counterbalance. I am of feeble constitution, and the doctors say that my lungs are affected. I have studied law, but the state of my health has obliged me to give up, for the present at least, the practice of my profession."

"But if you are rich you do not need to practice," said Herbert, who may be excused for still thinking his companion's lot a happy one.

"No, I do not need to practice my profession, so far as the earning of money is concerned; but I want something to occupy my mind. The doctors say I ought to take considerable out-door exercise; but I suppose my physical condition makes me indolent, for my chief exercise has been, thus far, to wander to the banks of the river and read under the trees."

"That isn't very severe exercise," said Herbert, smiling.

"No; still it keeps me out in the open air, and that is something. Now tell me, what are your plans?"

"My hope is to find something to do that will enable me to help mother; but there doesn't seem much chance of finding anything in Wayneboro. Do you think I could get a place in the city?"

"You might; but even if you did, you would find it difficult to earn your own living, and there would be no chance of your helping your mother."

Herbert, though naturally sanguine and hopeful, looked sober. Just then he had a bite, and drew out a good-sized pickerel. This gave a new direction to his thoughts, and he exclaimed, triumphantly:

"Look at this pickerel! He must weigh over two pounds."

"All of that," said the young man, rising and examining the fish with interest. "Let me use your pole, and see what luck I have."

"Certainly."

The young man, some ten minutes later, succeeded in catching a smaller pickerel, perhaps half the size of Herbert's.

"That will do for me," he said, "though it doesn't come up to your catch."

For two hours Herbert and his friend alternately used the pole, and the result was quite a handsome lot of fish.

"You have more fish than you want," said the young man. "You had better bring what you don't want to the hotel. I heard the landlord say he would like to buy some."

"That would suit me," said Herbert. "If he wants fish, I want money."

"Come along with me, then. Really, I don't know when I have passed a forenoon so pleasantly. Usually I get tired of my own company, and the day seems long to me. I believe I see my way clear to a better way of spending my time. You say you want a place. How would you like me for an employer?"

"I am sure I should like you, but you are not in any business."

"No," said the young man, smiling; "or, rather, my business is the pursuit of health and pleasure just now. In that I think you can help me."

"I shall be very glad to, if I can, Mr.——"

"My name is George Melville. Let me explain my idea to you. I want your company to relieve my solitude. In your company I shall have enterprise enough to go hunting and fishing, and follow out in good faith my doctor's directions. What do you say?"

Herbert smiled.

"I would like that better than being in the post office," he said. "It would seem like being paid for having a good time."

"How much would you consider your services worth?" asked Mr. Melville.

"I am content to leave that to you," said Herbert.

"Suppose we say six dollars a week, then?"

"Six dollars a week!" exclaimed Herbert, amazed.

"Isn't that enough?" asked Melville, smiling.

"It is more than I can earn. Mr. Graham thought he was over-paying me with three dollars a week."

"You will find me a different man from Mr. Graham, Herbert. I am aware that six dollars is larger pay than is generally given to boys of your age. But I can afford to pay it, and I have no doubt you will find the money useful."

"It will quite set us on our feet again, Mr. Melville," said Herbert, earnestly. "You are very generous."

"Oh, you don't know what a hard taskmaster you may find me," said the young man, playfully. "By the way, I consider that you have already entered upon your duties. To-day is the first day. Now come to the hotel with me, and see what you can get for the fish. I happen to know that two of the guests, a lady and her daughter, are anxious for a good fish dinner and, as there is no market here, I think the landlord will be glad to buy from you."

Mr. Melville was right. Mr. Barton, the landlord, purchased the fish that Herbert had to sell, for sixty cents, which he promptly paid.

"Don't that pay you for your morning's work?" asked Melville.

"I don't know but the money ought to go to you, Mr. Melville," said Herbert, "as I am now in your employ. Besides, you caught a part of them."

"I waive all claim to compensation," said the young man, "though it would be a novel sensation to receive money for services rendered. What will you say, Herbert, when I tell you that I never earned a dollar in my life?"

Herbert looked incredulous.

"It is really true," said George Melville, "my life has been passed at school and college, and I have never had occasion to work for money."

"You are in luck, then."

"I don't know that; I think those who work for the money they receive are happy. Tell me, now, don't you feel more satisfaction in the sixty cents you have just been paid because you have earned it?"

"Yes, sir."

"I thought so. The happiest men are those who are usefully employed. Don't forget that, and never sigh for the opportunity to lead an idle life. But I suppose your dinner is ready. You may go home, and come back at three o'clock."

"Very well, sir."

Herbert made good time going home. He was eager to tell his mother the good news of his engagement.

CHAPTER VII. EBEN GROWS ENVIOUS.

"Well, mother," said Herbert, as he entered the house, "I have brought you enough fish for dinner."

"I waited to see what luck you would have, Herbert, and therefore have not got dinner ready. You will have to wait a little while."

"I shall be all the hungrier, mother," said Herbert.

Mrs. Carr could not help noticing the beaming look on her som's face.

"You look as if you had received a legacy, Herbert," she said.

Herbert laughed.

"There it is," he said, displaying the sixty cents he had received from the landlord.

"There are ten cents more than I should have received for a whole day's work at the store," he said.

"Where did you get it, Herbert?"

"I sold a mess of fish to Mr. Barton, of the hotel."

"You must have had good luck in fishing," said his mother, looking pleased.

"I had help, mother. Mr. Melville, the young man from the city, who boards at the hotel, helped me fish."

"Well, Herbert, you have made a good beginning. I couldn't help feeling a little depressed when you left me this morning, reflecting that we had but my pension to depend upon. It seemed so unlucky that Eben Graham should have come home just at this time to deprive you of your place in the store."

"It was a piece of good luck for me, mother."

"I don't see how," said Mrs. Carr, naturally puzzled.

"Because I have a better situation already."

Then Herbert, who had been saving the best news for the last, told his mother of his engagement as Mr. Melville's companion, and the handsome compensation he was to receive.

"Six dollars a week!" repeated his mother. "That is indeed generous. Herbert, we did well to trust in Providence."

"Yes, mother; and we have not trusted in vain."

After dinner Herbert did some chores for his mother, and then went to the hotel to meet his new employer. He found him occupying a large and pleasant room on the second floor. The table near the window was covered with books, and there were some thirty or forty volumes arranged on shelves.

"I always bring books with me, Herbert," said the young man. "I am very fond of reading, and hitherto I have occupied too much time, perhaps, in that way—too much, because it has interfered with necessary exercise. Hereafter I shall devote my forenoon to some kind of outdoor exercise in your company, and in the afternoon you can read to me, or we can converse."

"Shall I read to you now, Mr. Melville?" asked Herbert.

"Yes; here is a recent magazine. I will select an article for you to read. It will rest my eyes, and besides it is pleasanter to have a companion than to read one's self."

The article was one that interested Herbert as well as Mr. Melville, and he was surprised when he had finished to find that it was nearly five o'clock.

"Didn't the reading tire you, Herbert?" asked Melville.

"No, sir; not at all."

"It is evident that your lungs are stronger than mine."

At five o'clock Melville dismissed his young companion.

"Do you wish me to come this evening?" asked Herbert.

"Oh, no. I wouldn't think of taking up your evenings."

"At the post office I had to stay till eight o'clock."

"Probably it was necessary there; I won't task you so much."

"When shall I come to-morrow?"

"At nine o'clock."

"That isn't very early," said Herbert, smiling.

"No, I don't get up very early. My health won't allow me to cultivate early rising. I shall not be through breakfast much before nine."

"I see you don't mean to overwork me, Mr. Melville."

"No, for it would involve overworking myself."

"I shall certainly have an easy time," thought Herbert, as he walked homeward.

He reflected with satisfaction that he was being paid at the rate of a dollar a day, which was quite beyond anything he had ever before earned. Indeed, to-day he had earned sixty cents besides. The sum received for the fish.

After supper Herbert went to the store to purchase some articles for his mother. He was waited on by Mr. Graham in person. As the articles called for would amount to nearly one dollar, the storekeeper said, cautiously: "Of course, you are prepared to pay cash?"

"Certainly, sir," returned Herbert.

"I mentioned it because I knew your income was small," said Ebenezer, apologetically.

"It is more than it was last week," said Herbert, rather enjoying the prospect of surprising the storekeeper.

"Why, you ain't found anything to do, have you?" asked Mr. Graham, his face indicating curiosity.

"Yes, sir; I am engaged as companion by Mr. Melville, who is staying at the hotel."

"I don't know what he wants of a companion," said the storekeeper, with that disposition to criticise the affairs of his neighbors often found in country places.

"He thinks he needs one," answered Herbert.

"And how much does he pay you now?" queried Ebenezer.

"Six dollars a week."

"You don't mean it!" ejaculated the storekeeper. "Why, the man must be crazy!"

"I don't think he is," said Herbert, smiling.

"Got plenty of money, I take it?" continued Ebenezer, who had a good share of curiosity.

"Yes; he tells me he is rich."

"How much money has he got?"

"He didn't tell me that."

"Well, I declare! You're lucky, that's a fact!"

There was an interested listener to this conversation in the person of Eben, who had been in the store all day, taking Herbert's place. As we know, the position by no means suited the young man. He had been employed in a store in Boston, and to come back to a small country grocery might certainly be considered a descent. Besides, the small compensation allowed him was far from satisfying Eben.

He was even more dissatisfied when he learned how fortunate Herbert was. To be selected as a companion by a rich young man was just what he would have liked himself, and he flattered himself that he should make a more desirable companion than a mere boy like Herbert.

As our hero was leaving the store, Eben called him back.

"What was that you were telling father about going round with a young man from the city?" he asked.

Herbert repeated it.

"And he pays you six dollars a week?" asked Eben, enviously.

"Yes; of course, I shouldn't have asked so much, but he fixed the price himself."

"You think he is very rich?" said Eben, thoughtfully.

"Yes, I think so."

"What a splendid chance it would be for me!" thought Eben. "If I could get intimate with a man like that, he might set me up in business some day; perhaps take me to Europe, or round the world!" "How much of the time do you expect to be with this Mr. Melville?" he asked.

Herbert answered the question.

"Does he seem like a man easy to get along with?"

"Very much so."

Eben inwardly decided that, if he could, he would oust Herbert from his desirable place, and substitute himself. It was a very mean thought, but Eben inherited meanness from his father.

"Herbert," he said, "will you do me a favor?"

"What is it?" asked our hero.

"Will you take my place in the store this evening? I am not feeling well, and want to take a walk."

"Yes," answered Herbert, "as soon as I have run home to tell mother where I am."

"That's a good fellow. You shan't lose anything by it. I'll give you ten cents."

"You needn't pay me anything, Eben. I'll do it as a favor."

"You're a trump, Herbert. Come back as soon as you can."

When Eben was released from the store, he went over to the hotel, and inquired for Mr. Melville, leaving his unsuspecting young substitute in the post office.

CHAPTER VIII. EBEN'S ASSURANCE.

"A young man wishes to see you, Mr. Melville," said the servant.

George Melville looked up in some surprise from his book, and said: "You may show him up."

"It must be Herbert," he thought.

But when the door was opened, and the visitor shown in, Mr. Melville found it was an older person than Herbert. Eben, for it was he, distorted his mean features into what he regarded as a pleasant smile, and, without waiting to receive a welcome, came forward with extended hand.

"I believe you are Mr. Melville," he said, inquiringly.

"Yes, that is my name," said Melville, looking puzzled; "I don't remember you. Have I met you before?"

"You saw me in father's store, very likely," said Eben. "I am Eben Graham, son of Ebenezer Graham, the postmaster."

"Indeed! That accounts for your face looking familiar. You resemble your father very closely."

"I'm a chip off the old block with modern improvements," said Eben, smirking. "Father's always lived in the country, and he ain't very stylish. I've been employed in Boston for a couple of years past, and got a little city polish."

"You don't show much of it," thought Melville, but he refrained from saying so.

"So you have come home to assist your father," he said, politely.

"Well, no, not exactly," answered Eben, "I feel that a country store isn't my sphere."

"Then you propose to go back to the city?"

"Probably I shall do so eventually, but I may stay here in Wayneboro a while if

I can make satisfactory arrangements. I assure you that it was not my wish to take Herbert Carr's place."

"Herbert told me that you had assumed his duties."

"It is only ad interim. I assure you, it is only ad interim. I am quite ready to give back the place to Herbert, who is better suited to it than I."

"I wonder what the fellow is driving at," thought Melville. Eben did not long leave him in doubt.

"Herbert tells me that he has made an engagement with you," continued Eben, desiring to come to his business as soon as possible.

"Yes, we have made a mutual arrangement."

"Of course, it is very nice for him; and so I told him."

"I think I am quite as much a gainer by it as he is," said Melville.

"Herbert was right. He is easily suited," said Eben, to himself.

"Of course," Eben added, clearing his throat, "Herbert isn't so much of a companion to you as if he were a few years older."

"I don't know that; it seems to me that he is a very pleasant companion, young as he is."

"To be sure, Herbert is a nice boy, and father was glad to help him along by giving him a place, with a larger salary than he ever paid before."

"What is he driving at?" thought Melville.

"To come to the point, Mr. Melville," said Eben, "I have made bold to call upon you to suggest a little difference in your arrangements."

"Indeed!" said Melville, coldly. Though he had no idea what his singular visitor was about to propose, it struck him emphatically that Eben was interfering in an unwarrantable manner with his affairs.

"You see," continued Eben, "I'm a good deal nearer your age than Herbert, and I've had the advantage of residing in the city, which Herbert hasn't, and naturally should be more company to you. Then, again, Herbert could do the work in the post office and store, which I am doing, nearly as well as I can. I'll undertake to get father to give him back his place, and then I shall be happy to make an arrangement with you to go hunting and fishing, or anything else that you choose. I am sure I should enjoy your company, Mr. Melville," concluded Eben, rubbing his hands complacently and surveying George Melville with an insinuating smile.

"You have certainly taken considerable trouble to arrange this matter for me," said Melville, with a sarcasm which Eben did not detect.

"Oh, no trouble at all!" said Eben, cheerfully. "You see, the idea came into my head when Herbert told me of his arrangements with you, and I thought I'd come and see you about it."

"Did you mention it to Herbert?" asked George Melville, with some curiosity.

"Well, no, I didn't. I didn't know how Herbert would look at it. I got Herbert to take my place in the store while I ran over to see you about the matter. By the way, though I am some years older than Herbert, I shan't ask more than you pay him. In fact, I am willing to leave the pay to your liberality."

"You are very considerate!" said Melville, hardly knowing whether to be amused or provoked by the cool assurance of his visitor.

"Oh, not at all!" returned Eben, complacently. "I guess I've fetched him!" he reflected, looking at Mr. Melville through his small, half-closed eyes.

"You have certainly surprised me very much, Mr. Graham," said Melville, "by the nature of your suggestion. I won't take into consideration the question whether you have thought more of your own pleasure or mine. So far as the latter is concerned, you have made a mistake in supposing that Herbert's youth is any drawback to his qualification as a companion. Indeed, his youth and cheerful temperament make him more attractive in my eyes. I hope, Mr. Graham, you will excuse me for saying that he suits me better than you possibly could."

Eben's countenance fell, and he looked quite discomfited and mortified.

"I didn't suppose a raw, country boy would be likely to suit a gentleman of taste, who has resided in the city," he said, with asperity.

"Then you will have a chance to correct your impression," said Melville, with a slight smile.

"Then you don't care to accept my offer?" said Eben, regretfully.

"Thank you, no. If you will excuse me for suggesting it, Mr. Graham, it would have been more considerate for you to have apprised Herbert of your object in asking him to take your place this evening. Probably he had no idea that you meant to supersede him with me."

Eben tossed his head.

"You mustn't think, Mr. Melville," he said, "that I was after the extra pay. Six dollars doesn't seem much to me. I was earning ten dollars a week in Boston, and if I had stayed, should probably have been raised to twelve."

"So that you were really consenting to a sacrifice in offering to enter my employment at six dollars a week?"

"Just so!"

"Then I am all the more convinced that I have decided for the best in retaining

Herbert. I do not wish to interfere with your prospects in the city."

"Oh, as for that," said Eben, judging that he had gone too far, "I don't care to go back to the city just yet. I've been confined pretty steadily, and a few weeks in the country, hunting and fishing, will do me good."

George Melville bowed, but said nothing.

Eben felt that he had no excuse for staying longer, and reluctantly rose.

"If you should think better of what I've proposed," he said, "you can let me know."

"I will do so," said Melville.

"He's rather a queer young man," muttered Eben, as he descended the stairs. "It's funny that he should prefer a country boy like Herbert to a young man like me who's seen life, and got some city polish—at the same price, too! He don't seem to see his own interest. I'm sorry, for it would have been a good deal more interesting to me, going round with him a few hours a day, than tending store for father. There's one thing sure, I won't do it long. I'm fitted for a higher position than that, I hope."

"For downright impudence and cool assurance, I think that young man will bear off the palm," thought George Melville, as his unwelcome visitor left the room. "Herbert is in no danger from him. It would probably surprise him if he knew that I should consider his company as an intolerable bore. I will tell Herbert to-morrow the good turn his friend has tried to do him."

CHAPTER IX. THE SOLITARY FARMHOUSE.

If Eben had been sensitive, the cool reception which he met with at the hands of Mr. Melville would have disturbed him. As it was, he felt angry and disappointed, and desirous of "coming up with" Herbert, as he expressed it, though it was hard to see in what way the boy had injured him. It did not seem quite clear at present how he was to punish Herbert, but he only waited for an occasion.

When Herbert learned, the next morning, from Mr. Melville, in what manner Eben had tried to undermine him, and deprive him of his situation, he was naturally indignant.

"I didn't think Eben Graham could be so mean," he exclaimed.

"It was certainly a mean thing to do, Herbert," said George Melville; "but you can afford to treat young Graham with contempt, as he has been unable to do you any injury."

"What shall we do this morning, Mr. Melville?" asked Herbert.

"I should like a row on the river," said Melville. "Do you know of any boat we can have?"

"Walter Ingalls has a boat; I think we can hire that."

"Do you know him?"

"Yes, sir."

"Then you may go and ascertain whether we can have it, or I will go with you to avoid loss of time."

The boat was readily loaned, and the two were soon on the river. Mr. Melville first took the oars, but he was quickly fatigued, and resigned them to Herbert, who was strong and muscular for his age. As his companion observed his strong and steady strokes, he said:

"Herbert, I am disposed to envy you your strength and endurance. I get tired very easily."

"Were you not strong when a boy?" asked Herbert.

"I never had much endurance. My mother had a feeble constitution and was consumptive, and I inherit something of her weakness."

"It is fortunate that you have money, Mr. Melville, so that you are not obliged to work."

"True; but I would give half my fortune to be strong and well."

Herbert noticed the hectic flush upon Mr. Melville's cheeks, and his white, transparent hands, and his sympathy was aroused.

"I see," he said, thoughtfully, "that I am more fortunate than I thought in my health and strength."

"They are blessings not to be overestimated, Herbert. However, my lot is, on the whole, a happy one, even though my life will probably be brief, and I have still many sources of satisfaction and enjoyment."

The river led away from the village, flowing between wooded banks, with here and there a cottage set in the midst of the fields. Lying back in the stern, Melville enjoyed their tranquil passage, when their attention was suddenly attracted by a boy who stood on the bank, frantically waving his hat. Melville was the first to see him.

"What can that boy want?" he asked.

Herbert immediately looked around, and exclaimed in surprise:

"It's Tom Tripp!"

"Row to shore, and see what he wants," said Melville, quickly.

They were already near, and in a brief space of time they touched the bank.

"What's the matter, Tom?"

"There's a tramp in the house, stealing all he can lay hands on," answered Tom, in excitement.

"What house?"

"Farmer Cole's."

Mr. Cole was the farmer for whom Tom Tripp was working.

Tom explained that the farmer was gone to the village, leaving his wife alone. A tramp had come to the door and asked for a meal. While Mrs. Cole was getting something for him, the visitor looked about him and, finding that there was no man about, boldly demanded money, after unceremoniously possessing himself of the silver spoons.

"Is he armed?" asked Melville.

"I don't know; I don't think so."

"Does he know that you have gone for help?"

"No; he did not see me. I came from the fields, and saw him through the window. Mrs. Cole thinks I am in the field and there is no help near."

Physical courage and physical strength do not always go together, and a weak man often excels a strong man in bravery. George Melville was thoroughly roused. For injustice or brutality he had a hearty contempt, and he was not one to stand by and see a ruffian triumph.

"Come, Herbert," he said; "let us go to the help of this poor woman."

"With all my heart," answered Herbert, his eyes flashing.

Before describing the appearance of Herbert and George Melville upon the scene, I will go back a few minutes and relate what happened at the farmhouse.

Mrs. Cole was engaged in ironing when she heard a knock at the door.

Answering the summons, she found herself confronted by an ill-looking fellow whose dusty and travel-soiled garments revealed the character of the wearer.

"What is it you wish?" asked the farmer's wife.

"I'm hungry!" said the tramp. "Can you give me something to eat?"

"Yes," answered Mrs. Cole, cheerfully, for the good woman could not find it in her heart to turn away a fellow creature suffering from hunger. "We have enough and to spare. Come in, and sit down at the table."

The visitor followed her into the kitchen and took a seat at the table, while the farmer's wife went to the pantry and brought out half a loaf of bread and a plate of cold meat.

The tramp was not long in attacking it, but after a few mouthfuls laid down his knife and fork.

"Where's the coffee?" he asked.

"I have no warm coffee," she answered.

"Don't you drink coffee in the morning?"

"Yes, but breakfast was over two or three hours since. Shall I get you a glass of water?"

"Haven't you any cider?"

"It seems to me you are particular," said Mrs. Cole, growing indignant.

"All the same I want some cider," said the tramp, impudently.

"I have no cider," answered Mrs. Cole, shortly.

"A pretty farmhouse this is, without cider," growled the tramp. "You can make me some coffee, then!"

"Who are you to order me round in my own house?" demanded Mrs. Cole, angrily. "One would think you took this for a hotel."

"I take it for what I please," said the tramp.

"If my husband were here you wouldn't dare to talk to me like this!"

It was an unguarded admission, made on the impulse of the moment, and Mrs. Cole felt its imprudence as soon as she had uttered the words, but it was too late to recall them.

"Where is your husband?" asked the tramp, his face lighting up with a gleam of exultation.

"Near by," answered Mrs. Cole, evasively; but her visitor saw that this was not correct.

"How much money have you in the house?" he demanded, abruptly.

"Money?" gasped the farmer's wife, turning pale.

"Yes, money! Didn't I speak plain enough?" asked the tramp, angrily.

"Are you a thief, then?"

"Don't you dare to call me a thief!" said the tramp, menacingly.

"Then, if you are an honest man, why do you ask that question?"

"Because I am going to borrow what money you have."

"Borrow!"

"Yes," said the man, with a grin. "I'll hand it back when I come around again."

Under ordinary circumstances there would not have been money enough in the farmhouse to be anxious about, but it so happened that Farmer Cole had sold a yoke of oxen, and the money received, a hundred dollars, was upstairs in a bureau drawer. The thought of this, though she didn't suppose the tramp to be aware of it, was enough to terrify Mrs. Cole, and she sank back in the chair in a panic. Of course the tramp inferred that there was a considerable sum in the house.

"Come, hurry up!" he said, roughly, "I can't wait here all day. Where do you keep the money?"

"It is my husband's," said Mrs. Cole, terrified out of all prudence.

"All right! I'll pay it back to him. While you're about it, you may collect all the spoons, too. I'm going to open a boarding house," he continued, with a chuckle, "and I shall need them."

"Oh, heavens! What shall I do?" ejaculated the frightened woman.

CHAPTER X. AN EXCITING SCENE.

"You'd better go upstairs and get that money, or I will go up myself," said the tramp, boldly.

"I will go," said Mrs. Cole, terrified.

It was at this time that Tom Tripp, looking in at the window, got an idea of the situation, but he was unobserved. The river bank was near, and he ran down to it, hoping, but not expecting, to see some one who could interfere with the impudent robber. We have already seen that he was luckier than he anticipated.

Meanwhile Mrs. Cole went upstairs, not knowing how to save the money from being carried away. She wished heartily that her husband had taken it with him. One hundred dollars, as she well knew, would be a serious loss to her husband, who was only moderately well to do. She thought it possible that the tramp might know how large a sum there was in the house, but could not be sure. She resolved, however, to make an effort to save the larger part of the money. From the wallet she took two five-dollar bills, and then, removing it from the drawer, put it between the beds. She lingered as long as she dared, and then went downstairs with the two bills in her hand.

"Well, have you got the money?" growled the tramp.

"Don't take it," she said; "be satisfied with the breakfast I have given you."

"You're a fool!" said the tramp, rudely. "How much have you got there?"

"Ten dollars."

"Ten dollars!" said the tramp, disdainfully. "What do you take me for?"

"It is a large sum of money to me and my husband, sir," said the poor woman, nervously.

"It isn't enough for me! You have got more money in the house. Don't lie to me! You know you have."

"I am not used to be talked to in that way," said Mrs. Cole, forgetting her timidity for the moment.

"I can't help what you are used to; you'd better not trifle with me. Go upstairs and bring down the rest of the money—do you hear?"

"Oh, sir!"

"'Oh, sir!'" repeated the tramp, impatiently. "I can't stay here all day. Are you going to do as I tell you?"

"I suppose I must," said the poor woman.

"That's sensible. You'll find out after a while that nothing is to be gained by trying to fool me. I'll give you just three minutes to find that money and bring it down."

"You'll leave the spoons, then?"

"No; I want them, as I've already told you. Come, two minutes are passed. I don't want to kill you, but—"

Mrs. Cole uttered a shriek of dismay, and turned to obey the command of her unwelcome visitor, when a loud, clear voice was heard from just outside the window.

"Stay where you are, Mrs. Cole! There is help at hand. This ruffian shall not harm you."

It was the voice of George Melville. The tramp turned swiftly and stared in ill-disguised dismay at Melville and Herbert.

"What business is it of yours?" he demanded, in a blustering tone.

"We make it our business to defend this lady from your thievish designs," said Melville.

"You!" exclaimed the tramp, contemptuously. "Why, I could twist either of you round my little finger."

"You'd better not try it!" said Melville, not showing the least trepidation. "Mrs. Cole, has this man anything of yours in his possession?"

"He has my spoons and I have just handed him ten dollars."

George Melville turned to the tramp.

"Be kind enough to lay the spoons on the table," he said, "and give back the ten dollars Mrs. Cole handed you."

"You must think I'm a fool!" said the tramp.

"No; but I think you are a prudent man. If you do as I say we will let you go; if not—"

"Well, if not?" blustered the tramp.

"If not, you may regret it."

All this time George Melville had spoken in his usual tone of voice, and the tramp was puzzled to know whether he had any weapon with him. For himself, he was unarmed, and this made him feel rather ill at ease, notwithstanding his superiority in physical strength. He was rather disposed to think that George Melville had a pistol, for he could not understand how otherwise he should dare to confront a man of twice his size and strength.

"I don't care for the spoons," he said, "but I will take the money."

"No, you will return the money," said Melville, calmly.

"Who will make me?" demanded the tramp, defiantly.

"I will."

"We'll see about that!" said the tramp, desperately, and he sprang towards Melville, who had in the meantime entered the house and stood only six feet distant.

"Stay where you are!" exclaimed Melville, resolutely, and he drew a pistol, which he leveled at his formidable antagonist.

"That settles it, stranger!" said the tramp, "You've got the advantage of me this time. Just wait till we meet again."

"I am willing to wait for some time," said Melville, shrugging his shoulders. "I have no desire to cultivate your acquaintance, my friend."

"There are the spoons!" said the tramp, throwing them down on the table.

"Now for the money!"

The tramp looked at George Melville. Melville still held the pistol in his hand leveled at his breast. The thief was a large man, but he was not a brave one. He cowered before the resolute glance of his small opponent.

"Won't you interfere with me if I give back the money?" he asked.

"No."

"Will you let me go without firing at me?"

"Yes."

"Perhaps you won't keep your agreement," suggested the tramp, nervously.

"I am a man of my word," said Melville, calmly.

His calm, resolute tone, free from all excitement, impressed the tramp with confidence. He drew the notes from his vest pocket, where he had thrust them, and threw them on the table.

"Now, may I go?" he said.

In answer, George Melville, who stood between him and the door, drew aside, still, however, holding the pistol in position, and the tramp passed out, not sorry, it may be said, to get out of range of the weapon.

They watched him striding through the yard, and when he was fairly gone Mrs. Cole said:

"Oh, how can I thank you for saving me from this wretch?"

"I am glad to have been the instrument of deliverance," said Melville, politely.

"It was fortunate you had the pistol with you, Mr. Melville," said Herbert.

"Well, yes, perhaps it was," said Melville, smiling.

"Pray, put it up, Mr. Melville," said the farmer's wife, "it always makes me nervous to see a loaded pistol."

Melville bowed, and put back the pistol in his pocket.

"As your unpleasant visitor has gone," he said, "I may as well relieve your fears by saying that the pistol is not loaded."

"Not loaded!" exclaimed Herbert and Tom Tripp in concert.

"No; it has not been loaded to my knowledge for a year."

"Then how could you stand up against that man?" asked the farmer's wife, in wonder.

"He thought it was loaded!" replied Melville, "and that answered the purpose. I should be very reluctant to use a loaded pistol, for I have a high idea of the sacredness of human life, but I have no objection to playing upon the fears of a man like that."

Melville and Herbert remained at the farmhouse for half an hour, till the return of the farmer, when they resumed their river trip. They returned about noon. When they were walking through the main street, Herbert saw the town constable approaching with the air of a man who had business with him.

"Did you wish to speak to me, Mr. Bruce?" he asked.

"Yes, Herbert. I have a warrant for your arrest."

"For my arrest!" exclaimed Herbert, in amazement. "What for?"

"On complaint of Eben Graham, for abstracting postage stamps and money from the post office last evening."

CHAPTER XI. TRIED FOR THEFT.

Herbert stared at the constable in blank amazement.

"I am charged with stealing stamps and money from the post office?" he said.

"Yes."

"Who makes the charge?" demanded Herbert, in great excitement.

"Eben Graham."

"I don't know what it means," said our hero, turning to George Melville.

"It means," said Melville, "that the fellow is envious of you, and angry because he cannot supersede you with me. He evidently wants to do you an injury."

"It must be so; but I did not imagine that Eben could be so mean. Mr. Bruce, do you believe that I am a thief?"

"No, I don't, Herbert," said the constable, "and it was very much against my will that I started out to arrest you, you may be sure."

"When do you want me to go with you?" asked Herbert.

"You will go before Justice Slocum at two o'clock."

"Is it necessary for me to go to the lockup?" asked Herbert, shrinking, with natural repugnance, from entering the temporary house of tramps and law breakers.

"No, Herbert," answered the constable, in a friendly tone. "I'll take it upon myself to let you go home to dinner. I will call for you at quarter of two. Of course I shall find you ready to accompany me?"

"Yes, Mr. Bruce, I am impatient to meet Eben Graham, and tell him to his face that he has been guilty of a mean and contemptible falsehood, in charging me with theft. Not a person in the village who knows me will believe it."

"I will also call at your house, Herbert," said George Melville, "and accompany you to the office of the justice. I shall ask leave to give the details of Eben Graham's visit to me last evening."

"Thank you, Mr. Melville," said Herbert, "I am glad you do not believe a word of this story."

"I am not so easily deceived, Herbert. It is quite possible that stamps and money have been stolen, but, if so, it is your false friend and accuser who is guilty."

Of course Herbert had to tell his mother what had happened. She was agitated and alarmed, but became calmer when Herbert told her what was Eben's probable motive in making the charge.

"How can he behave so shamefully!" exclaimed the indignant parent.

"I didn't think him capable of it, myself, mother, although I had a poor opinion of him."

"Suppose that you can't prove that you are innocent, Herbert?" said Mrs. Carr, anxiously.

"It is for him to prove that I am guilty, mother," answered Herbert, who knew this much of law.

At a quarter of two Constable Bruce and Mr. Melville walked to the house together.

The door was opened for them by Herbert himself.

"So you haven't taken leg bail, Herbert," said the constable, jocosely.

"No, Mr. Bruce, I am on hand; I am in a hurry to meet Mr. Eben Graham and see whether he can look me in the face after his shameful behavior."

"Oh, Mr. Bruce, I never thought you would call at my home on such an errand," said Mrs. Carr, on the point of breaking down.

"Don't worry, Mrs. Carr," said the constable; "anybody may be charged with theft, however innocent. Your son has good friends who won't see him treated with injustice."

Herbert's mother was desirous of accompanying them to the office of the justice, but was persuaded to remain behind. Herbert knew that in her indignation she would not be able to be silent when she saw Eben Graham.

Justice Slocum was an elderly man, with a mild face and gray hair. When Herbert entered he greeted him in a friendly way.

"I am sorry to see you here, my boy," he said, "but I am sure there is some mistake. I have known you ever since you were a baby, and I don't believe you are guilty of theft now."

"I submit, Judge Slocum," said Eben Graham, who sat in a corner, his mean features looking meaner and more insignificant than usual, "I submit that you are prejudging the case."

"Silence, sir!" said Judge Slocum, warmly. "How dare you impugn my conduct? Though Herbert were my own son, I would give you a chance to prove him guilty."

"I hope you'll excuse me, judge," said Eben, cringing. "I am as sorry as you are to believe the boy guilty of stealing."

"Do your worst and say your worst, Eben Graham!" said Herbert, contemptuously, "but be very careful that you do not swear falsely."

"I don't need any instructions from you, Herbert Carr, considering that you are a criminal on trial," said Eben, maliciously.

"You are mistaken, sir," said George Melville. "To be under arrest does not make a man or boy a criminal."

"I am sure I am much obliged for the information, Mr. Melville," said Eben, spitefully. "You've chosen a nice companion."

"There you are right," said Melville, gravely. "I have done much better than if I had hired you."

Eben winced, but did not reply.

George Melville whispered to Herbert:

"Are you willing to accept me as your lawyer? I am not much of one, to be sure, but this case is very simple."

"I am very grateful for your offer, and accept it," said Herbert.

I do not propose to record the whole scene in detail, but only to give a general idea of the proceedings.

Eben Graham was sworn as a witness, and deposed that he had left Herbert in charge of the post office the previous evening. On his return he examined the stamps and contents of the money drawer, and found, to his surprise, that five dollars in money and six dollars' worth of stamps were missing.

"How did you know they were missing?" asked Melville.

"Because I knew precisely how much money was in the drawer and how many stamps were there."

"Then you counted them just before you went out?"

"Yes, sir."

"That was rather a singular time to make the count, was it not?"

"I don't know that it was, sir."

"I should suppose the end of the day would be a more appropriate time."

"I don't think so," answered Eben, shortly.

"Were you led to make the count because you suspected Herbert's honesty?" asked Mr. Melville.

"That was the very reason I did it," said Eben, with a malicious glance at

Herbert.

"Isn't it a little curious that you should have selected a boy whose honesty you doubted, to fill your place?" asked George Melville, carelessly.

"There wasn't anybody else; he knew all about post-office work." answered Eben.

"Very good! Now, Mr. Graham, if you have no objection, will you tell why you wanted to get away from the post office last evening?"

Eben fidgeted, for he saw what was coming, and it made him nervous.

"I wanted a little rest," he answered, after a pause.

"Where did you go?"

"Why do you ask me that question?" asked Eben, moving about uneasily.

"Because I desire an answer."

"You know where I went," returned Eben, sullenly.

"Yes, but I wish you to tell me."

"Answer the question, witness!" said the judge, briefly.

"I went to the hotel," replied Eben, evasively.

"On whom did you call?"

"On you!" answered Eben, reluctantly.

"We have come to it at last. Now, what was your business with me?"

"To tell you that Herbert would not suit you as a companion," said the witness, who thought this answer rather a clever one.

"Whom did you recommend in his place?" pursued the questioner, relentlessly.

Eben hesitated, but his cleverness came again to his aid.

"I told you that I would be willing to come just to oblige you," he said.

"Did Herbert know that you were going to make this proposal?"

"No."

"You asked him, then, to remain in the post office while you absented yourself with a view of depriving him of the position he had just secured in my employ?"

"I would have got father to take him again in the store and post office," said Eben, defending himself from the implied charge of treachery.

"Yes, you told me so."

Eben nodded triumphantly. Even Melville had to admit that he was not treating Herbert meanly.

"By the way," said Melville, "isn't it rather strange that you should have been ready to recommend in your place a boy whose honesty you doubted?"

"I didn't know he was a thief," said Eben, somewhat abashed.

"No, but you suspected his honesty. That was your reason for counting the money and stamps before you left the office. At least, that is the reason you have given."

"He had been in the office before I was there," said Eben, uneasily.

"While he was there, were any stamps missing? Was he suspected of taking any stamps or money?"

"Not that I know of."

"Now, Mr. Graham, what answer did I make to your application?"

"What application?"

"To take you into my employ instead of Herbert."

"You wanted to keep him," said the witness, sullenly.

"Precisely. Having failed, then, in your application, you went home and discovered that some money and stamps had been stolen."

"Yes, sir. I was very much surprised—"

"That will do, sir. Your discovery was remarkably well-timed. Herbert having obtained the position you sought, you straightway discovered proof of his dishonesty."

Eben colored, for the insinuation was plain enough for even him to understand.

"The two things had nothing to do with each other!" he said.

"That may be, but I call the attention of the judge to a very remarkable coincidence. Have the missing stamps or money been found on the person of the defendant?"

"He hasn't been searched."

"I will take it upon me to say that he is ready to submit to an examination," said Melville.

Herbert said, emphatically, "I am."

"Oh, it isn't likely you'd find anything now." said Eben, with a sneer.

"Why not?"

"He has had plenty of time to put 'em away."

"I am willing to have my mother's house searched," said Herbert, promptly.

"Oh, they ain't there!" said Eben, significantly.

"Where are they, then?"

Eben's answer took Herbert and his lawyer, and the judge himself, by surprise.

CHAPTER XII. EBEN'S TRUMP CARD.

"I guess they're—a part of them—inside this letter," he said.

As he spoke he produced a letter, stamped and sealed, but not postmarked. The letter was addressed:

"Messrs. Jones & Fitch,

"—-Chestnut Street,

"Philadelphia."

"What makes you think this letter contains money or postage stamps, Mr. Graham?" asked George Melville.

"Because I've seen an advertisement of Jones & Fitch in one of the weekly papers. They advertise to send several articles to any address on receipt of seventy-five cents in postage stamps."

"Very well. What inference do you draw from this?"

"Don't you see?" answered Eben, in malicious triumph. "That's where part of the stamps went. This letter was put into the post office by Herbert Carr this morning."

"That is not true," said Herbert, quietly.

"Maybe it isn't, but I guess you'll find Herbert Carr's name signed to the letter," said Eben.

"Have you seen the inside of the letter, Mr. Graham?"

"No, sir."

"Then how do you know Herbert Carr's name is signed to it?"

"I don't know, but I am pretty sure it is."

"You think Herbert Carr wrote the letter?"

"Yes, sir."

"If there is no objection," said Melville, "I will settle the matter by opening it."

"That's what I want you to do." said Eben Graham.

"And I also," said Herbert.

Mr. Melville deliberately cut open one end of the envelope with a small penknife, and drew out the folded sheet which it contained. As he did so, a small sheet of postage stamps fell upon the floor.

"There, do you see that?" said Eben in triumph.

The sheet of stamps contained twenty-five three-cent stamps, representing in value seventy-five cents.

"Shall I read the letter, sir?" asked Melville, of the judge.

"If there is no objection."

Melville read it aloud, as follows:

"WAYNEBORO, August 2lst. MESSRS. JONES & FITCH: I inclose seventy-five cents in stamps, and will be glad to have you send me the articles you advertise in the Weekly Gazette. Yours truly,

"HERBERT CARR."

Herbert listened to the reading of this letter in amazement.

"I never wrote that letter," he said, "and I never heard of Jones & Fitch before."

"That's a likely story!" sneered Eben Graham. "I submit to Judge Slocum that I have proved my case. I haven't found out when all the stamps left, but I have shown where some are. One who will steal seventy-five cents' worth of stamps will steal six dollars' worth."

"I agree with you there, Mr. Graham," said George Melville. "Will you be kind enough to sit down at that table, and write to my dictation?"

"What should I do that for?" asked Eben, suspiciously.

"Never mind. Surely you can have no objection."

"Well, no; I don't know as I have, though I think it's all foolishness."

He sat down, and a pen was handed him.

"What shall I write?" he asked.

"Write 'Messrs. Jones & Fitch.'"

"What for?" demanded Eben, looking discomposed.

"That's my affair. Write."

Eben wrote the words, but he seemed to find some difficulty in doing so. It was clear that he was trying to disguise his handwriting.

"What next?" he asked.

"'I inclose seventy-five cents in stamps,'" proceeded George Melville.

"Do you want to throw suspicion on me?" asked Eben, throwing down the pen.

"Keep on writing!" said the judge.

Eben did so, but was very deliberate about it, and seemed very particular as to how he penned his letter.

"Very well!" said Melville. "Now, I wish Herbert Carr to take the pen, and I will dictate the same letter."

Herbert readily took the seat just vacated by Eben, and rapidly wrote the words dictated to him.

When he had finished his task, Mr. Melville took the two copies, and, first examining them himself, handed them, together with the original letter, to Justice Slocum.

"I have only to ask your honor," he said, "to compare these three notes and decide for yourself whether the original was written by Herbert Carr or Mr. Eben Graham, the witness against him."

Eben Graham looked very ill at ease, flushing and paling by turns while the examination was going on.

"I submit," he said, "that this is a very extraordinary way of treating a witness."

Justice Slocum, after a pause, said: "I find that Mr. Eben Graham's copy is unmistakably in the same handwriting as the original letter, purporting to be written by Herbert Carr."

"It's not so!" faltered Eben.

"Then," said George Melville, triumphantly, "as it seems clear that my young client is the victim of a base conspiracy, engineered by the man who has brought this charge of dishonesty against him, I have only to ask that he be honorably discharged."

"The request is granted," said Justice Slocum. "Herbert, you can go. It is clear that you are innocent of the charge made against you."

"I protest," began Eben Graham.

"As for you, Mr. Graham," said the justice, severely, "I have no words to express my scorn and detestation of your conduct in deliberately contriving a plot to ruin the reputation of an innocent boy, who has never done you any harm. Should Herbert Carr desire it, he is at liberty to sue you for having him arrested on a false charge trumped up by yourself."

Eben began to look frightened.

"I do not wish to punish Mr. Graham," said Herbert. "It is enough for me that my honesty has been vindicated."

"Go, then," said the justice to Eben. "It is fortunate for you that this boy is so forbearing."

Eben Graham slunk out of the justice's office, looking meaner and more contemptible than ever, while Herbert was surrounded by his friends, who congratulated him upon the happy issue of the trial.

CHAPTER XIII. EBEN'S LAST HOPE FAILS.

Ebenezer Graham had taken no stock in his son's charge against Herbert. He was not prejudiced in favor of Herbert, nor did he feel particularly friendly to him, but he was a man of shrewdness and common sense, and he knew that Herbert was not a fool. When Eben made known to him the fact that the stamps and money were missing, he said keenly: "What has become of 'em?"

"I don't know," answered Eben, "but I can guess well enough."

"Guess, then," said his father, shortly.

"You know Herbert Carr took my place last evening?"

"Well?"

"There's no doubt that he took the stamps and money."

"That isn't very likely."

"I feel sure of it—so sure that I mean to charge him with it."

"Well, you can see what he says."

Ebenezer did not understand that Eben intended to have the boy arrested, and would not have consented to it had he known. But Eben slipped out of the store, and arranged for the arrest without his father's knowledge. Indeed, he did not learn till the trial had already commenced, Eben having made some excuse for his absence.

When Eben returned his father greeted him in a tone very far from cordial.

"Well, Eben, I hear you've gone and made a fool of yourself?"

"I have only been defending your property, father," said Eben, sullenly. "I thought you'd appreciate it better than this."

"You've charged an innocent boy with theft, and now all his friends will lay it up agin' us."

"Were you going to be robbed without saying a word?" asked Eben.

"No, I'm not, Eben Graham; I'm goin' to say a word, and now's the time to say it. You can't pull wool over my eyes. The money's gone, and the stamps are gone, and somebody's got 'em."

"Herbert Carr!"

"No, it isn't Herbert Carr. It's somebody nearer to me, I'm ashamed to say, than Herbert Carr."

"Do you mean to say I took them?" asked Eben.

"I won't bring a charge unless I can prove it, but I shall watch you pretty closely after this."

"In that case, I don't wish to work for you any longer; I throw up the situation," said Eben, loftily.

"Very well. When are you going to leave town?"

"I ain't going to leave town at present."

"Where are you going to board, then?"

Eben regarded his father in dismay.

"You're not going to send me adrift, are you?" he asked, in consternation.

"I'm not going to support you in idleness; if you give up your situation in the store, you'll have to go to work for somebody else."

"I wish I could," thought Eben, thinking of the rich young man at the hotel, from whom he had sought a position as companion.

"Then I shall have to leave Wayneboro," he said; "there's nothing to do here."

"Yes, there is; Farmer Collins wants a hired man."

"A hired man!" repeated Eben, scornfully. "Do you think I am going—to hire out on a farm?"

"You might do a great deal worse," answered Ebenezer, sensibly.

"After being a dry-goods salesman in Boston, I haven't got down to that, I beg to assure you," said Eben, with an air of consequence.

"Then you will have to work in the store if you expect to stay at home," said his father. "And hark you, Eben Graham," he added, "don't report any more losses of money or stamps. I make you responsible for both."

Eben went back to his work in an uneasy frame of mind. He saw that he had not succeeded in imposing upon his father, and that the clear-sighted old gentleman strongly suspected where the missing articles had gone. Eben might have told, had he felt inclined, that the five-dollar bill had been mailed to a lottery agent in New York in payment for a ticket in a Southern lottery, and that the stamps were even now in his possession, and would be sold at the first opportunity. His plan to throw suspicion upon Herbert had utterly failed, and the cold looks with which he had been greeted showed what the villagers thought of his attempt.

"I won't stay in Wayneboro much longer," Eben inwardly resolved. "It's the dullest hole in creation. I can get along somehow in a large place, but here there's positively nothing. Hire out on a farm, indeed! My father ought to be ashamed to recommend such a thing to his only son, when he's so well off. If he would only give me two hundred dollars, I would go to California and trouble him no more. Plenty of people make money in California, and why shouldn't I? If that ticket draws a prize—"

And then Eben went into calculations of what he would do if only he drew a prize of a thousand dollars. That wasn't too much to expect, for there were several of that amount, and several considerably larger. He pictured how independent he would be with his prize, and how he would tell his father that he could get along without him, displaying at the same time a large roll of bills. When he reached California he could buy an interest in a mine, and perhaps within three or four years he could return home twenty times as rich as his father. It was pleasant to think over all this, and almost to persuade himself that the good luck had actually come. However, he must wait a few days, for the ticket had not yet come, and the lottery would not be drawn for a week.

The ticket arrived two days later; Eben took care to slip the envelope into his pocket without letting his father or anyone else see it, for unpleasant questions might have been asked as to where he got the money that paid for it, Mr. Graham knowing very well that his son had not five dollars by him.

For a few days Eben must remain in Wayneboro, until the lottery was drawn. If he was unlucky, he would have to consider some other plan for raising money to get away from Wayneboro.

It was not till the day after the trial and his triumphant acquittal, that Herbert saw Eben. He came to the store to buy some groceries for his mother.

"Good-evening, Herbert," said Eben.

"Eben," said Herbert, coldly, "except in the way of business, I don't want to speak to you."

"You don't bear malice on account of that little affair, do you, Herbert?" said Eben, smoothly.

"That little affair, as you call it, might have been a very serious affair to me."

"I only did my duty," said Eben.

"Was it your duty to charge an innocent person with theft?"

"I didn't see who else could have taken the things," said Eben.

"Probably you know as well as anybody," said Herbert, contemptuously.

"What do you mean?" demanded Eben, coloring.

"You know better than I do. How much do I owe you?"

"Thirty-three cents."

"There is your money," said Herbert, and walked out of the store.

"I hate that boy!" said Eben, scowling at Herbert's retreating figure. "He puts on too many airs, just because a city man's taken him in charity and is paying his expenses. Some time I'll be able to come up with him, I hope."

Herbert was not of an unforgiving nature, but he felt that Eben had wronged him deeply, and saw no reason why he would not repeat the injury if he ever got the chance. He had at least a partial understanding of Eben's mean nature and utter selfishness, and felt that he wished to have nothing to do with him. Ebenezer Graham was very "close," but he was a hard-working man and honest as the world goes. He was tolerably respected in Wayneboro, though not popular, but Eben seemed on the high road to become a rascal.

A week slipped by, and a circular containing the list of prizes drawn was sent to Eben.

He ran his eyes over it in a flutter of excitement. Alas! for his hopes. In the list of lucky numbers the number on his ticket was not included.

"I have drawn a blank! Curse the luck!" he muttered, savagely. "The old man needn't think I am going to stay here in Wayneboro. If he won't give me money to go out West, why, then—"

But he did not say what then.

CHAPTER XIV. A TRIP TO BOSTON.

"To-morrow, Herbert," said George Melville, as they parted for the day, "I shall propose a new excursion to you."

Herbert regarded him inquiringly.

"I want to go to Boston to make a few purchases, but principally to consult my physician."

"I hope you are not feeling any worse, Mr. Melville," said Herbert, with genuine concern, for he had come to feel a regard for his employer, who was always kind and considerate to him.

"No, I am feeling as well as usual; but I wish to consult Dr. Davies about the coming winter—whether he would advise me to spend it in Massachusetts."

"If Mr. Melville goes away, I shall have to look for another place," thought Herbert, soberly. It was hardly likely, he knew, that he would obtain a position so desirable as the one he now filled.

"I hope he will be able to do so, Mr. Melville," he said, earnestly.

"I hope so; but I shall not be surprised if the doctor ordered me away."

"Then you won't want me to come to-morrow?"

"Certainly, unless you object to going to Boston with me."

"Object?" repeated Herbert, eagerly. "I should like nothing better."

In fact, our hero, though a well-grown boy of sixteen, had never been to Boston but three times, and the trip, commonplace as it may seem to my traveled young readers, promised him a large amount of novelty and pleasurable excitement.

"I shall be glad of your company, Herbert. I hardly feel the strength or enterprise to travel alone, even for so trifling a trip as going to Boston."

"At what hour will you go, Mr. Melville?"

"I will take the second train, at nine o'clock. It will afford me time enough, and save my getting up before my usual time."

Herbert would have preferred going by the first train, starting at half-past seven, as it would have given him a longer day in the city, but of course he felt that his employer had decided wisely.

"It will be quite a treat to me, going to Boston," he said. "I have only been there three times in my life."

"You certainly have not been much of a traveler, Herbert," said George Melville, smiling. "However, you are young, and you may see a good deal of the world yet before you die."

"I hope I will. It must be delightful to travel."

"Yes, when you are young and strong," said Melville, thoughtfully. "That makes a great deal of difference in the enjoyment."

Herbert did not fail to put in an appearance at the hotel considerably before it was time to leave for the train. George Melville smiled at his punctuality.

"I wish, Herbert," he said, "that I could look forward with as much pleasure as you feel to our trip to-day."

"I wish so, too, Mr. Melville."

"At any rate, I shall enjoy it better for having a companion."

The tickets were bought, and they took their places in one of the passenger cars.

Just as the train was ready to start, Herbert saw a young man with a ticket in his hand hurrying along the platform.

"Why, there's Eben Graham!" he said, in surprise.

"Is he entering the cars?"

"Yes, he has just got into the car behind us."

"I wonder if he is going to leave Wayneboro for good?"

"Probably he is only going to Boston for the day, perhaps to buy goods."

Herbert thought it doubtful whether Ebenezer Graham would trust his son so far, but did not say so. Eben, on his part, had not seen Herbert on board the train, and was not aware that he was a fellow passenger.

The journey was a tolerably long one—forty miles—and consumed an hour and a half. At last they rolled into the depot, and before the train had fairly stopped the passengers began to crowd toward the doors of the car.

"Let us remain till the crowd has passed out," said George Melville. "It is disagreeable to me to get into the throng, and it saves very little time."

"Very well, sir."

Looking out of the car window, Herbert saw Eben Graham walking swiftly along the platform, and could not forbear wondering what had brought him to the city.

"My doctor's office is on Tremont Street," said Mr. Melville. "I shall go there immediately, and may have to wait some time. It will be tiresome to you, and I shall let you go where you please. You can meet me at the Parker House, in School Street, at two o'clock."

"Very well, sir."

"Do you know where the hotel is?"

"No, but I can find it," answered Herbert, confidently.

"I believe I will also get you to attend to a part of my business for me."

"I shall be very glad to do so," said Herbert, sincerely. It made him feel more important to be transacting business in Boston.

"Here is a check for a hundred and fifty dollars on the Merchants' Bank," continued George Melville. "It is payable to the bearer, and you will have no trouble in getting the money on it. You may present it at the bank, and ask for fives and tens and a few small bills."

"Very well, sir."

Herbert felt rather proud to have so much confidence reposed in him, for to him a hundred and fifty dollars seemed a large sum of money, and he felt that George Melville was a rich man to draw so much at one time.

"Had I better go to the bank at once?" he asked.

"Yes, I think so; of course, I need not caution you to take good care of the money."

"I'll be sure to do that, sir."

They walked together to Tremont Street, and Mr. Melville paused at a doorway opposite the Common.

"My doctor's office is upstairs," he said. "We will part here and meet at the hotel. If you are late, I may go into the dining room; so if you don't see me in the reading room, go to the door of the dining room and look in."

"Very well, sir; but I think I shall be on time."

"The bank is open now, and you can cash the check if you go down there."

Left to himself, Herbert walked slowly along, looking into shop windows and observing with interested attention the people whom he met.

"It must be very pleasant to live in the city," he thought; "there is so much going on all the time."

It is no wonder that country boys are drawn toward the city, and feel that their cup of happiness would be full if they could get a position in some city store. They do not always find the reality equal to their anticipations. The long hours and strict discipline of a city office or mercantile establishment are not much like the freedom they pictured to themselves, and after they have paid their board bill in some shabby boarding house they seldom find much left over, either for amusement or needful expenses. The majority of boys would do better to remain in their country homes, where at least they can live comfortably and at small expense, and take such employment as may fall in their way. They will stand a much better chance of reaching a competence in middle life than if they helped to crowd the ranks of city clerks and salesmen. There is many a hard-working clerk of middle age, living poorly, and with nothing laid by, in the city, who, had he remained in his native village, might have reached a modest independence. It was hardly to be expected, however, that Herbert would feel thus. Upon him the show and glitter of the city shops and streets produced their natural effect, and he walked on buoyantly, seeing three times as much as a city boy would have done.

He turned down School Street, passing the Parker House, where he was to meet Mr. Melville. Just before he reached it he saw Eben Graham emerge from the hotel and walk towards Washington Street. Eben did not look behind him, and therefore did not see Herbert.

"I wonder where he is going?" thought our hero, as he followed a few steps behind Eben.

CHAPTER XV. AN OBLIGING GUIDE.

On Washington Street, not far from Old South Church, is an office for the sale of railroad tickets to western points. It was this office which Eben entered.

"He is going to inquire the price of a ticket to some western city," thought Herbert. "I heard him say one day that he wanted to go West."

Our hero's curiosity was naturally aroused, and he stood at the entrance, where he could not only see but hear what passed within.

"What do you charge for a ticket to Chicago?" he heard Eben ask.

"Twenty-two dollars," was the answer of the young man behind the counter.

"You may give me one," said Eben.

As he spoke he drew from his vest pocket a roll of bills, and began to count off the requisite sum.

Herbert was surprised. He had supposed that Eben was merely making inquiries about the price of tickets. He had not imagined that he was really going.

"Can Mr. Graham have given him money to go?" he asked himself.

"When can I start?" asked Eben, as he received a string of tickets from the clerk.

"At three this afternoon."

Eben seemed well pleased with this reply. He carefully deposited the tickets in an inside vest pocket, and turned to go out of the office. As he emerged from it he caught sight of Herbert, who had not yet started to go. He looked surprised and annoyed.

"Herbert Carr!" he exclaimed. "How came you here?"

Mingled with his surprise there was a certain nervousness of manner, as Herbert thought.

"I came to Boston with Mr. Melville," said Herbert, coldly.

"Oh!" ejaculated Eben, with an air of perceptible relief. "Where is Mr. Melville?"

"He has gone to the office of his physician, on Tremont Street."

"Leaving you to your own devices, eh?"

"Yes."

"Look out you don't get lost!" said Eben, with affected gayety. "I am here on a little business for the old man."

Herbert did not believe this, in view of what he had seen, but he did not think it necessary to say so.

"Good-morning!" said Herbert, in a tone polite but not cordial.

"Good-morning! Oh, by the way, I have just been inquiring the cost of a ticket to St. Louis," said Eben, carelessly.

"Indeed! Do you think of going out there?"

"Yes, if the old man will let me," said Eben.

"Do you prefer St. Louis to Chicago?" asked Herbert, watching the face of Eben attentively.

Eben's face changed, and he looked searchingly at our hero, but could read nothing in his face.

"Oh, decidedly!" he answered, after a slight pause. "I don't think I would care for Chicago."

"And all the while you have a ticket for Chicago in your pocket!" thought Herbert, suspiciously, "Well, that's your own affair entirely, not mine."

"What train do you take back to Wayneboro?" asked Eben, not without anxiety.

"We shall not go before four o'clock."

"I may be on the train with you," said Eben, "though possibly I shall get through in time to take an earlier one."

"He is trying to deceive me," thought Herbert.

"Good-morning," he said, formally, and walked away.

"I wish I hadn't met him," muttered Eben to himself. "He may give the old man a clew. However, I shall be safe out of the way before anything can be done."

Herbert kept on his way, and found the bank without difficulty.

He entered and looked about him. Though unaccustomed to banks, he watched to see where others went to get checks cashed, and presented himself in turn.

"How will you have it?" asked the paying teller.

"Fives and tens, and a few small bills," answered Herbert, promptly.

The teller selected the requisite number of bank bills quickly, and passed them out to Herbert. Our hero counted them, to make sure that they were correct, and then put them away in his inside pocket. It gave him a feeling of responsibility to be carrying about so much money, and he felt that it was incumbent on him to be very careful.

"Where shall I go now?" he asked himself.

He would have liked to go to Charlestown, and ascend Bunker Hill Monument, but did not know how to go. Besides, he feared he would not get back to the Parker House at the time fixed by Mr. Melville. Still, he might be able to do it. He addressed himself to a rather sprucely dressed man of thirty-five whom he met at the door of the bank.

"I beg your pardon, sir, but can you tell me how far it is to Bunker Hill Monument?"

"About a mile and a half," answered the stranger.

"Could I go there and get back to the Parker House before one o'clock."

"Could you?" repeated the man, briskly. "Why, to be sure you could!"

"But I don't know the way."

"You have only to take one of the Charlestown horse cars, and it will land you only a couple of minutes' walk from the monument."

"Can you tell me what time it is, sir?"

"Only a little past eleven. So you have never been to Bunker Hill Monument, my lad?"

"No sir; I live in the country, forty miles away and seldom come to Boston."

"I see, I see," said the stranger, his eyes snapping in a very peculiar way. "Every patriotic young American ought to see the place where Warren fell."

"I should like to if you could tell me where to take the cars."

"Why, certainly I will," said the other, quickly. "In fact—let me see," and he pulled out a silver watch from his vest pocket, "I've a great mind to go over with you myself."

"I shouldn't like to trouble you, sir," said Herbert.

"Oh, it will be no trouble. Business isn't pressing this morning, and I haven't been over for a long time myself. If you don't object to my company, I will accompany you."

"You are very kind," said Herbert. "If you are quite sure that you are not inconveniencing yourself, I shall be very glad to go with you—that is, if you think I can get back to the Parker House by one o'clock."

"I will guarantee that you do," said the stranger, confidently. "My young friend, I am glad to see that you are particular to keep your business engagements. In a varied business experience, I have observed that it is precisely that class who are destined to win the favor of their employer and attain solid success."

"He seems a very sensible man," thought Herbert; "and his advice is certainly good."

"Come this way," said the stranger, crossing Washington Street. "Scollay's Square is close at hand, and there we shall find a Charlestown horse car."

Of course Herbert yielded himself to the guidance of his new friend, and they walked up Court Street together.

"That," said the stranger, pointing out a large, somber building to the left, "is the courthouse. The last time I entered it was to be present at the trial of a young man of my acquaintance who had fallen into evil courses, and, yielding to temptation, had stolen from his employer. It was a sad sight," said the stranger, shaking his head.

"I should think it must have been," said Herbert.

"Oh, why, why will young men yield to the seductions of pleasure?" exclaimed the stranger, feelingly.

"Was he convicted?" asked Herbert.

"Yes, and sentenced to a three years term in the State prison," answered his companion. "It always makes me feel sad when I think of the fate of that young man."

"I should think it would, sir."

"I have mentioned it as a warning to one who is just beginning life," continued the stranger. "But here is our car."

A Charlestown car, with an outside sign, Bunker Hill, in large letters, came by, and the two got on board.

They rode down Cornhill, and presently the stranger pointed out Faneuil Hall.

"Behold the Cradle of Liberty," he said. "Of course, you have heard of Faneuil Hall?"

"Yes, sir," and Herbert gazed with interest at the building of which he had heard so much.

It was but a short ride to Charlestown. They got out at the foot of a steep street, at the head of which the tall, granite column which crowns the summit of Bunker Hill stood like a giant sentinel ever on guard.

CHAPTER XVI. A NEW BATTLE OF BUNKER HILL.

Just opposite the monument is a small, one-story structure, where views of the shaft may be purchased and tickets obtained.

"There is a small admission fee," said Herbert's companion.

"How much is it?" asked our hero.

"Twenty cents."

As Herbert thrust his hand into his pocket for the necessary money, his companion said:

"You had better let me pay for both tickets."

Though he said this, he didn't make any motion to do so.

"No, I will pay for both," said Herbert.

"But I really cannot permit you to pay for mine."

And still the speaker made no movement to purchase his ticket.

Herbert settled the matter by laying half a dollar on the desk, and asking for two tickets. He began to see that, in spite of his disclaimer, his guide intended him to do so. On the whole, this didn't please him. He would rather have had his offer frankly accepted.

"I didn't mean to have you pay," said the young man, as they passed through the door admitting them to an inner apartment, from which there was an exit into a small, inclosed yard, through which they were to reach the entrance to a spiral staircase by which the ascent was made.

Herbert did not answer, for he understood that his guide was not telling the truth, and he did not like falsehood or deceit.

They entered the monument and commenced the ascent.

"We have a tiresome ascent before us," said the other.

"How many steps are there?" asked Herbert.

"About three hundred," was the reply.

At different points in the ascent they came to landings where they could catch glimpses of the outward world through long, narrow, perpendicular slits in the sides of the monument.

At last they reached the top.

Herbert's guide looked about him sharply, and seemed disappointed to find a lady and gentleman and child also enjoying the view.

Herbert had never been so high before. Indeed, he had never been in any high building, and he looked about him with a novel sense of enjoyment.

"What a fine view there is here!" he said.

"True," assented his companion. "Let me point out to you the different towns visible to the naked eye."

"I wish you would," said the boy.

So his guide pointed out Cambridge, Chelsea, Malden, the Charles and Mystic

Rivers, gleaming in the sunshine, the glittering dome of the Boston State House and other conspicuous objects. Herbert felt that it was worth something to have a companion who could do him this service, and he felt the extra twenty cents he had paid for his companion's ticket was a judicious investment.

He noticed with some surprise that his companion seemed annoyed by the presence of the other party already referred to. He scowled and shrugged his shoulders when he looked at them, and in a low voice, inaudible to those of whom he spoke, he said to Herbert: "Are they going to stay here all day?"

"What does it matter to me if they do?" returned Herbert, in surprise.

Indeed, to him they seemed very pleasant people, and he was especially attracted by the sweet face of the little girl. He wished he had been fortunate enough to possess such a sister.

At last, however, they finished their sightseeing, and prepared to descend. Herbert's companion waited till the sound of their descending steps died away, and then, turning to Herbert, said in a quick, stern tone: "Now give me the money you have in your pocket."

"What do you mean?" he said.

Herbert recoiled, and stared at the speaker in undisguised astonishment.

"I mean just what I say," returned the other. "You have one hundred and fifty dollars in your pocket. You need not deny it, for I saw you draw it from the bank and put it away."

"Are you a thief, then?" demanded Herbert.

"No matter what I am, I must have that money," said the stranger. "I came over with you exclusively to get it, and I mean business."

He made a step towards Herbert, but the boy faced him unflinchingly, and answered resolutely: "I mean business, too. The money is not mine, and I shall not give it up."

"Take care!" said the other, menacingly, "we are alone here. You are a boy and I am a man."

"I know that; but you will have to fight to get the money," said Herbert, without quailing.

He looked to the staircase, but his treacherous guide stood between him and it, and he was practically a prisoner at the top of the monument.

"Don't be a fool!" said the stranger. "You may as well give up the money to me first as last."

"I don't propose to give it up to you at all," said Herbert. "My employer trusted me with it, and I mean to be true to my trust."

"You can tell him that it was taken from you—that you could not help yourself. Now hand it over!"

"Never!" exclaimed Herbert, resolutely.

"We'll see about that," said his companion, seizing the boy and grappling with him.

Herbert was a strong boy for his age, and he accepted the challenge. Though his antagonist was a man, he found that the boy was powerful, and not to be mastered as easily as he anticipated.

"Confound you!" he muttered, "I wish I had a knife!"

Though Herbert made a vigorous resistance, his opponent was his superior in strength, and would ultimately have got the better of him. He had thrown Herbert down, and was trying to thrust his hand into his coat pocket, when a step was heard, and a tall man of Western appearance stepped on the scene.

"Hello!" he said, surveying the two combatants in surprise. "What's all this? Let that boy alone, you skunk, you!"

As he spoke, he seized the man by the collar and jerked him to his feet.

"What does all this mean?" he asked, turning from one to the other.

"This boy has robbed me of one hundred and fifty dollars," said the man, glibly. "I fell in with him in the Boston cars, and he relieved me of a roll of bills which I had drawn from a bank in Boston."

"What have you got to say to this?" asked the Western man, turning to Herbert, who was now on his feet.

"Only this," answered Herbert, "that it is a lie. It was I who drew the money from the Merchants' Bank in Boston. This man saw me cash the check, followed me, and offered to come here with me, when I asked him for directions."

"That's a likely story!" sneered the young man. "My friend here is too sharp to believe it."

"Don't call me your friend!" said the Western man, bluntly. "I'm more than half convinced you're a scamp."

"I don't propose to stay here and be insulted. Let the boy give me my money, and I won't have him arrested."

"Don't be in too much of a hurry, young man! I want to see about this thing. What bank did you draw the money from?"

"From the Merchants' Bank—the boy has got things reversed. He saw me draw it, inveigled himself into my confidence, and picked my pocket."

"Look here—stop right there! Your story doesn't hang together!" said the tall Westerner, holding up his finger. "You said you met this boy in a horse car."

"We came over together in a Charlestown horse car," said the rogue, abashed.

"You've given yourself away. Now make yourself scarce! Scoot!"

The rascal looked in the face of the tall, resolute man from the West, and thought it prudent to obey. He started to descend, but a well-planted kick accelerated his progress, and he fell down several steps, bruising his knees.

"Thank you, sir!" said Herbert, gratefully. "It was lucky you came up just as you did. The rascal had got his hand on the money."

"He is a miserable scamp!" answered Herbert's new friend. "If there'd been a police-man handy, I'd have given him in charge. I've come clear from Wisconsin to see where Warren fell, but I didn't expect to come across such a critter as that on Bunker Hill."

Herbert pointed out to his new friend the objects in view, repeating the information he had so recently acquired. Then, feeling that he could spare no more time, he descended the stairs and jumped on board a horse car bound for Boston.

CHAPTER XVII. AN ACCEPTABLE PRESENT.

As the clock at the Old South Church struck one, Herbert ascended the steps of Parker's Hotel, and walked into the reading room. George Melville was already there.

"You are on time, Herbert," he said, with a smile, as our hero made his appearance.

"Yes, sir; but I began to think I should miss my appointment."

"Where have you been?"

"To Bunker Hill."

"Did you ascend the monument?"

"Yes, sir, and had a fight at the summit."

Mr. Melville looked at Herbert in amazement.

"Had a fight at the top of Bunker Hill Monument?" he ejaculated.

"Yes, sir; let me tell you about it."

When the story was told, Mr. Melville said: "That was certainly a remarkable adventure, Herbert. Still, I am not sorry that it occurred."

It was Herbert's turn to look surprised.

"I will tell you why. It proves to me that you are worthy of my confidence, and can be trusted with the care of money. It has also taught you a lesson, to beware of knaves, no matter how plausible they may be."

"I haven't got over my surprise yet, sir, at discovering the real character of the man who went with me. I am sorry I met him. I don't like to distrust people."

"Nor I. But it is not necessary to distrust everybody. In your journey through the world you will make many agreeable and trustworthy acquaintances in whom it will be safe to confide. It is only necessary to be cautious and not give your confidence too soon."

"Oh, I didn't mention that I met somebody from Wayneboro," said Herbert.

"Was it Eben Graham?"

"Yes."

"I met him myself on Washington Street. Did you speak to him?"

"Yes, sir."

"I suppose he goes back to-night?"

"I don't think he will go back at all, Mr. Melville."

His employer looked at him inquiringly.

"I saw him buy a ticket to Chicago, though he does not know it," continued Herbert. "When he spoke with me he didn't admit it, but spoke of going back by an afternoon train."

"I am afraid he has appropriated some of his father's funds," said Melville. "I doubt if Ebenezer Graham would voluntarily furnish him the means of going West."

"That was just what occurred to me," said Herbert; "but I didn't like to think that Eben would steal."

"Perhaps he has not. We shall be likely to hear when we return. But you must be hungry. We will go in to dinner."

Herbert followed Mr. Melville into the dining room, where a good dinner was ordered, and partaken of. Herbert looked over the bill of fare, but the high prices quite startled him. He was not used to patronizing hotels, and it seemed to him that the price asked for a single dish ought to be enough to pay for a whole dinner for two. He knew about what it cost for a meal at home, and did not dream that it would amount to so much more at a hotel.

When the check was brought Herbert looked at it.

"Two dollars and a half!" he exclaimed.

"It costs an awful amount to live in Boston."

"Oh a dinner can be got much cheaper at most places in Boston," said George Melville, smiling, "but I am used to Parker's, and generally come here."

"I am glad it doesn't cost so much to live in Wayneboro," said Herbert. "We couldn't afford even one meal a day."

"You haven't asked me what the doctor said," remarked Melville, as they left the dining room.

"Excuse me, Mr. Melville. It wasn't from any lack of interest."

"He advises me to go West by the first of October, either to Colorado or Southern California."

Herbert's countenance fell. The first of October would soon come, and his pleasant and profitable engagement with Mr. Melville would close.

"I am sorry," he said, gravely.

"I am not so sorry as I should have been a few weeks ago," said Melville. "Then I should have looked forward to a journey as lonely and monotonous. Now, with a companion, I think I may have a pleasant time."

"Who is going with you, Mr. Melville?" asked Herbert, feeling, it must be confessed, a slight twinge of jealousy.

"I thought perhaps you would be willing to accompany me," said Melville.

"Would you really take me, Mr. Melville?" cried Herbert, joyfully.

"Yes, if you will go."

"I should like nothing better. I have always wanted to travel. It quite takes my breath away to think of going so far away."

"I should hardly venture to go alone," continued George Melville. "I shall need some one to look after the details of the journey, and to look after me if I fall sick. Do you think you would be willing to do that?"

"I hope you won't fall sick, Mr. Melville; but if you do, I will take the best care of you I know how."

"I am sure you will, Herbert, and I would rather have you about me than a man. Indeed, I already begin to think of you as a younger brother."

"Thank you, Mr. Melville," said Herbert, gratefully. "I am glad you do."

"Do you think your mother will object to your leaving home, Herbert?"

"Not with you. She knows I shall be well provided for with you. Can I arrange to send money regularly to mother?" asked the boy. "I shouldn't like to think of her as suffering for want of it."

"Yes, but to guard against emergencies, we can leave her a sum of money before you start."

After dinner Mr. Melville proposed to Herbert to accompany him on a walk up Washington Street, They walked slowly, Herbert using his eyes diligently, for to him the display in the shop windows was novel and attractive.

At length they paused at the door of a large and handsome jewelry store—one of the two finest in Boston.

"I want to go in here, Herbert," said his employer.

"Shall I stay outside?"

"No, come in with me. You may like to look about."

Though Herbert had no idea of the cost of the fine stock with which the store was provided, he saw that it must be valuable, and wondered where purchasers enough could be found to justify keeping so large a supply of watches, chains, rings and the numberless other articles in gold and silver which he saw around him.

"I would like to look at your watches," said Melville to the salesman who came forward to inquire his wishes.

"Gold or silver, sir?"

"Silver."

"This way, if you please."

He led the way to a case where through the glass covering Herbert saw dozens of silver watches of all sizes and grades lying ready for inspection.

"For what price can I get a fair silver watch?" asked Melville.

"Swiss or Waltham?"

"Waltham. I may as well patronize home manufactures."

"Here is a watch I will sell you for fifteen dollars," said the salesman, drawing out a neat-looking watch, of medium size. "It will keep excellent time, and give you good satisfaction."

"Very well; I will buy it on your recommendation. Have you any silver chains?"

One was selected of pretty pattern, and George Melville paid for both.

"How do you like the watch and chain, Herbert?" said his employer, as they left the store.

"They are very pretty, sir."

"I suppose you wonder what I want of two watches," said Melville.

"Perhaps you don't like to take your gold watch with you when you go out

West, for fear of thieves."

"No, that is not the reason. If I am so unfortunate as to lose my gold watch, I will buy another. The fact is, I have bought this silver watch and chain for you."

"For me!" exclaimed Herbert, intensely delighted.

"Yes; it will be convenient for you, as well as me, to be provided with a watch. Every traveler needs one. There; put it in your pocket, and see how it looks."

"You are very kind to me, Mr. Melville," said Herbert, gratefully. "You couldn't have bought me anything which I should value more."

When Herbert had arranged the watch and chain to suit him, it must be confessed that it engrossed a large part of his attention, and it was wonderful how often he had occasion to consult it during the first walk after it came into his possession.

CHAPTER XVIII. A THIEF IN TROUBLE.

"Have you ever visited the suburbs of Boston?" asked Melville.

"No," answered Herbert. "I know very little of the city, and nothing of the towns near it."

"Then, as we have time to spare, we will board the next horse car and ride out to Roxbury."

"I should like it very much, Mr. Melville," said Herbert, in a tone of satisfaction. I may remark that Roxbury was at that time a separate municipality, and had not been annexed to Boston.

They did not have to wait long for a car. An open car, of the kind in common use during the pleasant season, drew near, and they secured seats in it. After leaving Dover Street, Washington Street, still then narrow, broadens into a wide avenue, and is called the Neck. It was gay with vehicles of all sorts, and Herbert found much to attract his attention.

"The doctor tells me I ought to be a good deal in the open air," said Melville, "and I thought I would act at once upon his suggestion. It is much pleasanter than taking medicine."

"I should think so," answered Herbert, emphatically.

Arrived at the end of the route, Melville and Herbert remained on the car, and returned at once to the city. When they reached the crowded part of Washington Street a surprise awaited Herbert.

From a small jewelry store they saw a man come out, and walk rapidly away.

"Mr. Melville," said Herbert, in excitement, "do you see that man?"

"Yes. What of him?"

"It is the man who tried to rob me on Bunker Hill Monument."

He had hardly uttered these words when another man darted from the shop, bareheaded, and pursued Herbert's morning acquaintance, crying, "Stop, thief!"

The thief took to his heels, but a policeman was at hand, and seized him by the collar.

"What has this man been doing?" he asked, as the jeweler's clerk came up, panting.

"He has stolen a diamond ring from the counter," answered the clerk. "I think he has a watch besides."

"It's a lie!" said the thief, boldly.

"Search him!" said the clerk, "and you'll find that I have made no mistake."

"Come with me to the station house, and prepare your complaint," said the policeman.

By this time a crowd had gathered, and the thief appealed to them.

"Gentlemen," he said, "I am a reputable citizen of St. Louis, come to Boston to buy goods, and I protest against this outrage. It is either a mistake or a conspiracy, I don't know which."

The thief was well dressed, and some of the bystanders were disposed to put confidence in him. He had not seen Herbert and George Melville, who had left the car and joined the throng, or he might not have spoken so confidently.

"He doesn't look like a thief," said one of the bystanders, a benevolent-looking old gentleman.

"I should say not," said the thief, more boldly. "It's a pretty state of things if a respectable merchant can't enter a store here in Boston without being insulted and charged with theft. If I only had some of my friends or acquaintances here, they would tell you that it is simply ridiculous to make such a charge against me."

"You can explain this at the station house," said the policeman. "It is my duty to take you there."

"Is there no one who knows the gentleman?" said the philanthropist before referred to. "Is there no one to speak up for him?"

Herbert pressed forward, and said, quietly:

"I know something of him; I passed the morning in his company."

The thief turned quickly, but he didn't seem gratified to see Herbert.

"The boy is mistaken," he said, hurriedly; "I never saw him before."

"But I have seen you, sir," retorted our hero. "You saw me draw some money from a bank in State Street, scraped acquaintance with me, and tried to rob me of it on Bunker Hill."

"It's a lie!" said the prisoner, hoarsely.

"Do you wish to make a charge to that effect?" asked the policeman.

"No, sir; I only mentioned what I knew of him to support the charge of this gentleman," indicating the jeweler's clerk.

The old gentleman appeared to lose his interest in the prisoner after Herbert's statement, and he was escorted without further delay to the station house, where a gold watch and the diamond ring were both found on his person. It is scarcely needful to add that he was tried and sentenced to a term of imprisonment in the very city—Charlestown—where he had attempted to rob Herbert.

"It is not always that retribution so quickly overtakes the wrongdoer," said Melville. "St. Louis will hardly be proud of the man who claims her citizenship."

"Dishonesty doesn't seem to pay in his case," said Herbert, thoughtfully.

"It never pays in any case, Herbert," said George Melville, emphatically. "Even if a man could steal enough to live upon, and were sure not to be found out, he would not enjoy his ill-gotten gain, as an honest man enjoys the money he works hard for. But when we add the risk of detection and the severe penalty of imprisonment, it seems a fatal mistake for any man to overstep the bounds of honesty and enroll himself as a criminal."

"I agree with you, Mr. Melville," said Herbert, thoughtfully. "I don't think I shall ever be tempted, but if I am, I will think of this man and his quick detection."

When they reached the depot, a little before four o'clock, George Melville sent Herbert to the ticket office to purchase tickets, while he remained in the waiting room.

"I might as well accustom you to the duties that are likely to devolve upon you," he said, with a smile.

Herbert had purchased the tickets and was turning away, when to his surprise he saw Ebenezer Graham enter the depot, laboring evidently under considerable excitement. He did not see Herbert, so occupied was he with thoughts of an unpleasant nature, till the boy greeted him respectfully.

"Herbert Carr!" he said; "when did you come into Boston?"

"This morning, sir."

"Have you seen anything of my son, Eben, here?" gasped Mr. Graham.

"Yes, sir; he was on the same train, but I did not see him to speak to him till after I reached the city."

"Do you know what he has been doing here?" asked Ebenezer, his face haggard with anxiety.

"I only saw him for five minutes," answered Herbert, reluctant to tell the father what he knew would confirm any suspicion he might entertain.

"Where did you see him?" demanded Ebenezer, quickly.

"At a railroad ticket office not far from the Old South Church."

"Do you know if he bought any ticket?" asked Ebenezer, anxiously.

"Yes," answered Herbert. "I overheard him purchasing a ticket to Chicago."

Ebenezer groaned, and his face seemed more and more wizened and puckered up.

"It is as I thought!" he exclaimed, bitterly. "My own son has robbed me and fled like a thief, as he is."

Herbert was shocked, but not surprised. He didn't like to ask particulars, but Ebenezer volunteered them.

"This morning," he said, "I foolishly gave Eben a hundred dollars, and sent him to Boston to pay for a bill of goods which I recently bought of a wholesale house on Milk Street. If I had only known you were going in, I would have sent it by you."

Herbert felt gratified at this manifestation of confidence, especially as he had so recently been charged with robbing the post office, but did not interrupt Mr. Graham, who continued:

"As soon as Eben was fairly gone, I began to feel sorry I sent him, for he got into extravagant ways when he was in Boston before, and he had been teasing me to give him money enough to go out West with. About noon I discovered that he had taken fifty dollars more than the amount I intrusted to him, and then I couldn't rest till I was on my way to Boston to find out the worst. I went to the house on Milk Street and found they had seen nothing of Eben. Then I knew what had happened. The graceless boy has robbed his father of a hundred and fifty dollars, and is probably on his way West by this time."

"He was to start by the three o'clock train, I think," said Herbert, and gave his reasons for thinking so.

Ebenezer seemed so utterly cast down by this confirmation of his worst suspicions, that Herbert called Mr. Melville, thinking he might be able to say something to comfort him.

CHAPTER XIX. EBENEZER GRAHAM'S GRIEF.

"How much have you lost by your son, Mr. Graham?" asked George Melville.

"Nearly two hundred and fifty dollars," groaned Ebenezer, "counting what I paid in the city to his creditors, it is terrible, terrible!" and he wrung his hands in his bitterness of spirit.

"I am sorry for you," said Melville, "and still more for him."

"Why should you be sorry for him?" demanded Ebenezer, sharply. "He hasn't lost anything."

"Is it nothing to lose his consciousness of integrity, to leave his home knowing that he is a thief?"

"Little he'll care for that!" said Mr. Graham, shrugging his shoulders. "He's laughing in his sleeve, most likely, at the way he has duped and cheated me, his father."

"How old is Eben, Mr. Graham?"

"He will be twenty in November," answered Ebenezer, apparently puzzled by the question.

"Then, as he is so young, let us hope that he may see the error of his ways, and repent."

"That won't bring me back my money," objected Ebenezer, querulously. It was clear that he thought more of the money he had lost than of his son's lack of principle.

"No, it will not give you back your money, but it may give you back a son purified and prepared to take an honorable position in society."

"No, no; he's bad, bad!" said the stricken father. "What did he care for the labor and toil it took to save up that money?"

"I hope the loss of the money will not distress you, Mr. Graham."

"Well, no, not exactly," said Ebenezer, hesitating. "I shall have to take some money from the savings bank to make up what that graceless boy has stolen."

It was clear that Ebenezer Graham would not have to go to the poorhouse in consequence of his losses.

"I can hardly offer you consolation," said George Melville, "but I suspect that you will not be called upon to pay any more money for your son."

"I don't mean to!" said Ebenezer, grimly.

"Going away as he has done, he will find it necessary to support himself, and will hardly have courage to send to you for assistance."

"Let him try it!" said Ebenezer, his eyes snapping.

"He may, therefore, being thrown upon his own resources, be compelled to work hard, and that will probably be the best thing that can happen to him."

"I hope he will! I hope he will!" said the storekeeper. "He may find out after a while that he had an easy time at home, and was better paid than he will be among strangers. I won't pay any more of his debts. I'll publish a notice saying that I have given him his time, and won't pay any more debts of his contracting. He might run into debt enough to ruin me, between now and the time he becomes of age."

George Melville considered that the storekeeper was justified in taking this step, and said so.

While they were on the train, Ebenezer got measurably reconciled to his loss, and his busy brain began to calculate how much money he would save by ceasing to be responsible for Eben's expenses of living and prospective debts. Without this drawback, he knew he would grow richer every year. He knew also that notwithstanding the sum it had just cost him, he would be better off at the end of the year than the beginning, and to a man of his character this was perhaps the best form of consolation that he could have.

Suddenly it occurred to Mr. Graham that he should need a clerk in place of his son.

"Now that Eben has gone, Herbert," he said, "I am ready to take you back."

This was a surprise, for Herbert had not thought of the effect upon his own business prospects.

"I have got a place, thank you, Mr. Graham," he said.

"You don't call trampin' round huntin' and fishin' work, do you?" said Ebenezer.

"It is very agreeable work, sir."

"But it stands to reason that you can't earn much that way. I wouldn't give you twenty-five cents a week for such doings."

"Are you willing to pay me more than Mr. Melville does?" asked Herbert, demurely, smiling to himself.

"How much does he pay you now?" asked Ebenezer, cautiously.

"Six dollars a week."

"Six dollars a week!" repeated the storekeeper, in incredulous amazement.

"Sho! you're joking!"

"You can ask Mr. Melville, sir."

Ebenezer regarded George Melville with an inquiring look.

"Yes, I pay Herbert six dollars a week," said he, smiling.

"Well, I never!" ejaculated Ebenezer. "That's the strangest thing I ever heard. How in the name of conscience can a boy earn so much money trampin' round?"

"Perhaps it would not be worth as much to anyone else," said Melville, "but Herbert suits me, and I need cheerful company."

"You ain't goin' to keep him long at that figger, be you, Mr. Melville?" asked Mr. Graham, bluntly.

"I think we shall be together a considerable time, Mr. Graham. If, however, you should be willing to pay Herbert a larger salary, I might feel it only just to release him from his engagement to me."

"Me pay more'n six dollars a week!" gasped Ebenezer. "I ain't quite crazy. Why, it would take about all I get from the post office."

"You wouldn't expect me to take less than I can earn elsewhere, Mr. Graham," said Herbert.

"No-o!" answered the storekeeper, slowly. He was evidently nonplused by the absolute necessity of getting another clerk, and his inability to think of a suitable person.

"If Tom Tripp was with me, I might work him into the business," said Ebenezer, thoughtfully, "but he's bound out to a farmer."

An inspiration came to Herbert. He knew that his mother would be glad to earn something, and there was little else to do in Wayneboro.

"I think," he said, "you might make an arrangement with my mother, to make up and sort the mail, for a time, at least."

"Why, so I could; I didn't think of that," answered Ebenezer, relieved. "Do you think she'd come over to-morrow mornin'?"

"If she can't, I will," said Herbert. "I don't meet Mr. Melville till nine o'clock."

"So do! I'll expect you. I guess I'll come over and see your mother this evenin', and see if I can't come to some arrangement with her."

It may be added that Mr. Graham did as proposed, and Mrs. Carr agreed to render him the assistance he needed for three dollars a week. It required only her mornings, and a couple of hours at the close of the afternoon, and she was very glad to convert so much time into money.

"It makes me feel more independent," she said. "I don't want to feel that you do all the work, Herbert, and maintain the family single-handed."

The same evening Herbert broached the plan of traveling with Mr. Melville. As might have been expected, his mother was at first startled, and disposed to object, but Herbert set before her the advantages, both to himself and the family, and touched upon the young man's need of a companion so skillfully and eloquently that she was at last brought to regard the proposal favorably. She felt that George Melville was one to whom she could safely trust her only boy. Moreover, her own time would be partly occupied, owing to the arrangement she had just made to assist in the post office, so that Herbert carried his point.

The tenth of October arrived, the date which George Melville had fixed upon for his departure. Mrs. Carr had put Herbert's wardrobe in order, and he had bought himself a capacious carpetbag and an umbrella, and looked forward with eagerness to the day on which their journey was to commence. He had long thought and dreamed of the West, its plains and cities, but had never supposed that it would be his privilege to make acquaintance with them, at any rate, until he should have become twice his present age. But the unexpected had happened, and on Monday he and George Melville were to start for Chicago.

CHAPTER XX. AN OLD ACQUAINTANCE IN CHICAGO.

In due time our travelers reached Chicago, and put up at the Palmer House. Herbert was much impressed by the elegance of the hotel, its sumptuous furniture, and luxurious table. It must be considered that he was an inexperienced traveler, though had he been otherwise he might be excused for his admiration.

"I have some business in Chicago, and shall remain two or three days," said George Melville.

Herbert was quite reconciled to the delay, and, as his services were not required, employed his time in making himself familiar with the famous Western city. He kept his eyes open, and found something new and interesting at every step. One day, as he was passing through the lower portion of the city, his attention was called to a young man wheeling a barrow of cabbages and other vegetables, a little in advance of him. Of course, there was nothing singular about this, but there seemed something familiar in the figure of the young man. Herbert quickened his step, and soon came up with him.

One glance was enough. Though disguised by a pair of overalls, and without a coat, Herbert recognized the once spruce dry-goods clerk, Eben Graham.

Eben recognized Herbert at the same time. He started, and flushed with shame, not because of the theft of which he had been guilty, but because he was detected in an honest, but plebeian labor.

"Herbert Carr!" he exclaimed, stopping short.

"Yes, Eben; it is I!"

"You find me changed," said Eben, dolefully.

"No, I should recognize you anywhere."

"I don't mean that. I have sunk very low," and he glanced pathetically at the wheelbarrow.

"If you refer to your employment, I don't agree with you. It is an honest business."

"True, but I never dreamed when I stood behind the counter in Boston, and waited on fashionable ladies, that I should ever come to this."

"He seems more ashamed of wheeling vegetables than of stealing," thought Herbert, and he was correct.

"How do you happen to be in this business, Eben?" he asked, with some curiosity.

"I must do it or starve. I was cheated out of my money soon after I came here, and didn't know where to turn."

Eben did not explain that he lost his money in a gambling house. He might have been cheated out of it, but it was his own fault, for venturing into competition with older and more experienced knaves than himself.

"I went for thirty-six hours without food," continued Eben, "when I fell in with a man who kept a vegetable store, and he offered to employ me. I have been with him ever since."

"You were fortunate to find employment," said Herbert.

"Fortunate!" repeated Eben, in a tragic tone. "How much wages do you think I get?"

"I can't guess."

"Five dollars a week, and have to find myself," answered Eben, mournfully. "What would my fashionable friends in Boston say if they could see me?"

"I wouldn't mind what they said as long as you are getting an honest living."

"How do you happen to be out here?" asked Eben.

His story was told in a few words.

"You are always in luck!" said Eben, enviously. "I wish I had your chance. Is Mr. Melville very rich?"

"He is rich; but I don't know how rich."

"Do you think he'd lend me money enough to get home?"

"I don't know."

"Will you ask him?"

"I will tell him that you made the request, Eben," answered Herbert, cautiously. "Have you applied to your father?"

"To the old man? Yes. He hasn't any more heart than a grindstone," said Eben, bitterly. "What do you think he wrote me?"

"He refused, I suppose."

"Here is his letter," said Eben, drawing from his pocket a greasy half sheet of note paper. "See what he has to say to his only son."

This was the letter:

"EBEN GRAHAM: I have received your letter, and am not surprised to hear that you are in trouble. 'As a man sows, so also shall he reap.' A young man who will rob his father of his hard earnings is capable of anything. You have done what you could to ruin me, and deserve what you have got. You want me to send you money to come home, and continue your wicked work—I shall not do it. I wash my hands of you; I have already given notice, through the country paper that I have given you your time, and shall pay no more debts of your contracting.

"I am glad to hear that you are engaged in an honest employment. It is better than I expected. I would not have been surprised if I had heard that you were in jail. My advice to you is to stay where you are and make yourself useful to your employer. He may in time raise your wages. Five years hence, if you have turned over a new leaf and led an honest life, I may give you a place in my store. At present, I would rather leave you where you are.

"EBENEZER GRAHAM."

"What do you say to that? Isn't that rather rough on an only son, eh?" said Eben.

It occurred to Herbert that Eben hardly deserved very liberal treatment from his father, notwithstanding he was an only son.

"Oh, the old man is awfully mean and close-fisted," said Eben. "He cares more for money than for anything else. By the way, how does Melville treat you?"

"Mr. Melville," said Herbert, emphasizing the Mr., "is always kind and considerate."

"Pays you well, eh?"

"He pays me more than I could get anywhere else."

"Pays all your hotel and traveling expenses, eh?"

"Of course."

"And a good salary besides?"

"Yes."

"Herbert," said Eben, suddenly, "I want you to do me a favor."

"What is it?"

"You've always known me, you know. When you was a little chap, and came into the store, I used to give you sticks of candy."

"I don't remember it," answered Herbert, truthfully.

"I did, all the same. You were so young that you don't remember it."

"Well, Eben, what of it?"

"I want you to lend me ten dollars, Herbert, in memory of old times."

Herbert was generously inclined, on ordinary occasions, but did not feel so on this occasion. He felt that Eben was not a deserving object, even had he felt able to make so large a loan. Besides, he could not forget that the young man who now asked a favor had brought a false charge of stealing against him.

"You will have to excuse me, Eben," he answered. "To begin with, I cannot afford to lend so large a sum."

"I would pay you back as soon as I could."

"Perhaps you would," said Herbert, "though I have not much confidence in it. But you seem to forget that you charged me with stealing only a short time since. I wonder how you have the face to ask me to lend you ten dollars, or any sum."

"It was a mistake," muttered Eben, showing some signs of confusion.

"At any rate, I won't say anything more about it while you are in trouble. But you must excuse my declining to lend you."

"Lend me five dollars, then," pleaded Eben.

"What do you want to do with it?"

"To buy lottery tickets. I am almost sure I should win a prize, and then I can pay you five dollars for one."

"I wouldn't lend any money for that purpose to my dearest friend," said Herbert "Buying lottery tickets is about the most foolish investment you could make."

"Then I won't buy any," said Eben. "Lend me the money and I will use it to buy clothes."

"You will have to excuse me," said Herbert, coldly.

"I didn't think you'd be so mean," whined Eben, "to a friend in distress."

"I don't look upon you as a friend, and for very good reasons," retorted Herbert, as he walked away.

Eben looked after him with a scowl of hatred.

"I'd like to humble that boy's pride," he muttered, as he slowly resumed his march.

CHAPTER XXI. COL. WARNER.

When Herbert returned to the hotel he found George Melville in the reading room in conversation with a tall and dignified-looking stranger.

"Is that your brother, Mr. Melville?" asked the latter, as Herbert came forward and spoke to Melville.

"No, Colonel, he is my young friend and confidential clerk, Herbert Carr."

"Glad to make your acquaintance, Mr. Carr," said the colonel, affably, extending his hand as he spoke.

"This is Col. Warner, Herbert," explained George Melville.

Herbert, who was naturally polite, shook hands with the colonel, and said he was glad to make his acquaintance.

"I have been talking with Mr. Melville," said the colonel. "I am sorry to hear that he is traveling in search of health."

"Yes, sir; I hope he will find his journey beneficial."

"Oh, not a doubt of it! Not a doubt of it! I've been there myself. Do you know, when I was twenty-five, which I take to be about the age of your employer, I thought I should die of consumption?"

"I shouldn't have supposed it, sir," said Herbert, and Melville, too, felt surprised, as he noticed the stalwart proportions of the former consumptive.

"Ha! ha! I dare say not," said the colonel, laughing. "I don't look much like it now, eh?"

"No, you certainly don't, colonel," said Melville. "I am curious to know how you overcame the threatened danger."

"I did what you are doing, sir; I came West."

"But the mere coming West did not cure you, did it?"

"No, sir; it was the life I lived," returned Col. \Varner. "I didn't stay in the cities; I went into the wilderness. I lived in a log-cabin. I bought a horse, and rode every day. I kept in the open air, and, after a while, I found my strength returning and my chest expanding, and in a twelvemonth I could afford to laugh at doctors."

"And you have never had a return of the old symptoms?" asked Melville, with interest.

"Never, except four years afterwards, when I went to New York and remained nearly a year. I am now fifty, and rather hale and hearty for my years, eh?"

"Decidedly so."

"Let me advise you to follow my example, Mr. Melville."

"It was my intention when I started West to live very much as you indicated," said Melville. "Now that I have heard your experience, I am confirmed in my resolve."

"Good! I am glad to hear it. When do you leave Chicago?"

"To-morrow, probably."

"And how far West do you intend to go?"

"I have thought of Colorado."

"Couldn't do better. I know Colorado like a book. In fact, I own some valuable mining property there, up in—ahem! Gilpin County. By the way—I take it you are a rich man—why don't you invest in that way? Perhaps, however, you have it in view?"

"No, I haven't thought of it," answered Melville. "The fact is, I am not anxious to become richer, having enough for all my present needs."

"Just so," said the colonel. "But you might marry."

"Even if I did—"

"You would have money enough," said Col. Warner, finishing the sentence for him. "Well, I am delighted to hear it. I am very well fixed myself—in fact, some of my friends call me, ha! ha!—the nabob. But, as I was saying I am rich enough and to spare, and still—you may be surprised—still I have no objection to making a little more money."

Col. Warner nodded his head vigorously, and watched George Melville to see the effect upon him of this extraordinary statement.

"Very natural, colonel," said Melville. "I believe most people want to be richer. Perhaps if I had vigorous health I might have the same wish. At present my chief wish is to recover my health."

"You'll do it, sir, you'll do it—and in short order, too! Then you can turn your attention to money-making."

"Perhaps so," said Melville, with a smile.

"If not for yourself, for your young friend here," added the colonel. "I take it he is not rich."

"I have my fortune still to make, Col. Warner," said Herbert, smiling.

"The easiest thing in the world out here, my boy!" said the colonel, paternally. "So you start to-morrow?" he inquired, turning to Melville.

"I think of it."

"Egad! I've a great mind to accompany you," said the colonel. "Why shouldn't I? I've got through all my business in Chicago, and I like the pure air of the prairies best."

"We shall be glad of your company, colonel," said Melville, politely.

"Thank you, sir; that decides me. I'll see you again and fix the hour of going, or rather I'll conform myself to your arrangements."

"Very well, colonel."

"What do you think of my new acquaintance, Col. Warner, Herbert?" asked Melville when they were alone.

"He seems to have a very good opinion of himself," answered Herbert.

"Yes, he is very well pleased with himself. He isn't a man exactly to my taste, but he seems a representative Western man. He does not look much like a consumptive?"

"No, sir."

"I feel an interest in him on that account," said Melville, seriously. "If at any time I could become as strong and stalwart I would willingly surrender one-half, nay nine-tenths of my fortune. Ill health is a great drag upon a man; it largely curtails his enjoyments, and deprives him of all ambition."

"I don't see why his remedy wouldn't work well in your case, Mr. Melville," said Herbert, earnestly.

"Perhaps it may. At any rate, I feel inclined to try it. I am glad the colonel is going to travel with us, as I shall be able to question him about the details of his cure. He seems a bluff, genial fellow, and though I don't expect to enjoy his companionship much, I hope to derive some benefit from it."

"By the way, Mr. Melville, I met an old acquaintance while I was out walking," said Herbert.

"Indeed!"

"Eben Graham."

"How did he look—prosperous?"

"Hardly—he was wheeling a barrow of vegetables."

"Did you speak with him?"

"Yes; he wanted to borrow money."

"I am not surprised at that; I thought it time for him to be out of money. Did you lend him?"

"No; I found he wanted money to buy a lottery ticket. I told him I wouldn't lend money to my best friend for that purpose."

"Very sensible in you, Herbert."

"If he had been in distress, I might have let him have a few dollars, notwithstanding he treated me so meanly at Wayneboro, but he seems to be earning a living."

"I presume he doesn't enjoy the business he is in?"

"No; he complains that he has lowered himself by accepting such a place."

"It doesn't occur to him that he lowered himself when he stole money from his father, I suppose."

"It doesn't seem to."

Later in the day Herbert came across Col. Warner in the corridor of the hotel.

"Ha! my young friend!" he said, affably. "I am glad to meet you."

"Thank you, sir."

"And how is your friend?"

"No change since morning," answered Herbert, slightly smiling.

"By the way, Herbert—your name is Herbert, isn't it—may I offer you a cigar?" said Col. Warner.

The colonel opened his cigar-case and extended it to Herbert.

"Thank you, sir, but I don't smoke."

"Don't smoke? That is, you don't smoke cigars. May I offer you a cigarette?"

"I don't smoke at all, colonel."

"Indeed, remarkable! Why, sir, before I was your age I smoked."

"Do you think it good for consumption?" asked Herbert.

"Ha, ha, you have me there! Well, perhaps not. Do you know," said the colonel, changing the conversation, "I feel a great interest in your friend."

"You are very kind."

"'Upon my soul, I do. He is a most interesting young man. Rich, too! I am glad he is rich!"

"He would value health more than money," said Herbert.

"To be sure, to be sure! By the way, you don't know how much property your friend has?"

"No, sir, he never told me," answered Herbert, surprised at the question.

"Keeps such matters close, eh? Now, I don't. I never hesitate to own up to a quarter of a million. Yes, quarter of a million! That's the size of my pile."

"You are fortunate, Col. Warner," said Herbert, sincerely.

"So I am, so I am! Two years hence I shall have half a million, if all goes well. So you won't have a cigar; no? Well, I'll see you later."

"He's a strange man," thought Herbert. "I wonder if his statements can be relied upon." Somehow Herbert doubted it. He was beginning to distrust the colonel.

CHAPTER XXII. A MOUNTAIN STAGE.

We pass over several days, and change the scene. We left Herbert and Melville in the Palmer House in Chicago, surrounded by stately edifices and surging crowds. Now everything is changed. They are in a mountainous district, where a man might ride twenty miles without seeing a house. They are, in fact, within the limits of what was then known as the Territory of Colorado. It is not generally known that Colorado contains over a hundred mountain summits over ten thousand feet above the sea level. It is perhaps on account of the general elevation that it is recommended by physicians as a good health resort for all who are troubled with lung complaints.

At the time of which I speak most of the traveling was done by stage. Now railroads unite the different portions with links of steel, and make traveling less cumbersome and laborious. There was one of the party, however, who did not complain, but rather enjoyed the jolting of the lumbering stage-coach.

Col. Warner was of the party. He professed to feel an extraordinary interest in George Melville, and was anxious to show him the country where he had himself regained his health.

"Lonely, sir!" repeated the colonel, in answer to a remark of George Melville. "Why, sir, it's a populous city compared with what it was in '55, when I was out here. I built myself a cabin in the woods, and once for twelve months I didn't see a white face."

"Were there many Indians, Colonel?" asked Herbert.

"Indians? I should say so. Only twenty miles from my cabin was an Indian village."

"Did they trouble you any?" asked Herbert, curiously.

"Well, they tried to," answered the colonel. "One night as I lay awake I heard stealthy steps outside, and peeping through a crevice between the logs just above the head of my bed—by the way, my bed was the skin of a bear I had myself killed—I could see a string of Utes preparing to besiege me."

"Were you afraid?" asked Herbert, a little mischievously, for he knew pretty well what the colonel would say.

"Afraid!" repeated the colonel, indignantly. "What do you take me for? I have plenty of faults," continued Col. Warner, modestly, "but cowardice isn't one of them. No, sir; I never yet saw the human being, white, black, or red, that I stood in fear of. But, as I was saying, the redskins collected around my cabin, and were preparing to break in the door, when I leveled my revolver and brought down their foremost man. This threw them into confusion. They retreated a little way, then advanced again with a horrible yell, and I gave myself up for lost. But I got in another shot, bringing down another warrior, this time the son of their chief. The same scene was repeated. Well, to make a long story short, I repulsed them at every advance, and finally when but three were left, they concluded that prudence was the better part of valor, and fled, leaving their dead and wounded behind them."

"How many were there of them?" asked Herbert.

"Well, in the morning when I went out I found seven dead redskins, and two others lying at the point of death."

"That was certainly a thrilling adventure, Colonel," said George Melville, smiling.

"Egad, I should say so."

"I confess I don't care to meet with any such."

"Oh, no danger, no danger!" said the colonel, airily. "That is, comparatively speaking. In fact, the chief danger is of a different sort."

"Of the sleigh upsetting and tipping us out into some of the canyons, I suppose you mean?"

"No, I speak of the gentlemen of the road—road agents as they are generally called."

"You mean highwaymen?"

"Yes."

"Is there much danger of meeting them?" asked Melville.

"Well, there's a chance. They are quite in the habit of attacking stage-coaches, and plundering the passengers. Sometimes they make rich hauls."

"That must be rather inconvenient to the passengers." said Melville. "Can't the laws reach these outlaws?"

"They don't seem to. Why, there are men who have been in the business for years, and have never been caught."

"Very true," said a fellow traveler. "There's Jerry Lane, for instance. He has succeeded thus far in eluding the vigilance of the authorities."

"Yes," said the colonel, "I once saw Lane myself. Indeed he did me the honor of relieving me of five hundred dollars."

"Couldn't you help it?" asked Herbert.

"No; he covered me with his revolver, and if I had drawn mine I shouldn't have lived to take aim at him."

"Were you in a stage at the time?"

"No, I was riding on horseback."

"Is this Lane a large man?" asked George Melville.

"Not larger than myself," continued the colonel.

"Where does he live—in some secret haunt in the forest, I suppose?"

"Oh, no, he doesn't confine himself to one place. He travels a good deal. Sometimes he goes to St. Louis. I have heard that he sometimes even visits New York."

"And is he not recognized?"

"No; he looks like anything but an outlaw. If you should see him you might think him a prosperous merchant, or banker."

"That's curious!" said Herbert.

"The fact is," said the colonel, "when you travel by stage-coaches in these solitudes you have to take the chances. Now I carry my money concealed in an inner pocket, where it isn't very likely to be found. Of course I have another wallet, just for show, and I give that up when I have to."

There was a stout, florid gentleman present, who listened to the above conversation with ill-disguised nervousness. He was a New York capitalist, of German birth, going out to inspect a mine in which he proposed purchasing an interest. His name was Conrad Stiefel.

"Good gracious!" said he, "I had no idea a man ran such a risk, or I would have stayed at home. I decidedly object to being robbed."

"Men are robbed in a different way in New York," said George Melville.

"How do you mean, Mr. Melville?"

"By defaulting clerks, absconding cashiers, swindlers of excellent social position."

"Oh, we don't mind those things," said Mr. Stiefel. "We can look out for ourselves. But when a man points at you with a revolver, that is terrible!"

"I hope, my dear sir, you take good care of your money."

"That I do," said Stiefel, complacently. "I carry it in a belt around my waist. That's a good place, hey?"

"I commend your prudence, sir," said the colonel. "You are evidently a wise and judicious man."

"They won't think of looking there, hey?" laughed Stiefel.

"I should say not."

"You may think what you like, Mr. Stiefel," said a tall, thin passenger, who looked like a book peddler, "but I contend that my money is in a safer place than yours."

"Indeed, Mr. Parker, I should like to know where you keep it," said Col. Warner, pleasantly.

"You can't get at it without taking off my stockings," said the tall man, looking about him in a self-satisfied manner.

"Very good, 'pon my soul!" said the colonel. "I really don't know but I shall adopt your hiding place. I am an old traveler, but not too old to adopt new ideas when I meet with good ones."

"I think you would find it to your interest, Colonel," said Parker, looking flattered.

"Well, well," said the colonel, genially, "suppose we change the subject. There isn't much chance of our being called upon to produce our money, or part with it. Still, as I said a while since, it's best to be cautious, and I see that you all are so. I begin to feel hungry, gentlemen. How is it with you?"

"Are we anywhere near the place for supper?" asked Stiefel. "I wish I could step into a good Broadway restaurant; I feel empty."

"Only a mile hence, gentlemen, we shall reach Echo Gulch, where we halt for the night. There's a rude cabin there, where they will provide us with supper and shelter."

This announcement gave general satisfaction. The colonel proved to be right. The stage soon drew up in front of a long one-story building, which bore the pretentious name of the Echo Gulch Hotel.

CHAPTER XXIII. A STARTLING REVELATION.

A stout, black-bearded man stood in front of the hotel to welcome the stage passengers. He took a clay pipe from his lips and nodded a welcome.

"Glad to see you, strangers," he said. "Here, Peter, you black rascal, help the gentlemen with their baggage."

The door was thrown open, and the party filed into a comfortless looking apartment, at one end of which was a rude bar.

One of the passengers, at least, seemed to know the landlord, for Col. Warner advanced to greet him, his face beaming with cordiality.

"How are you, John?" he said. "How does the world use you?"

The landlord growled something inaudible.

"Have a drink, colonel?" was the first audible remark.

"Don't care if I do. It's confounded dry traveling over these mountain roads. Walk up, gentlemen. Col. Warner doesn't drink alone."

With the exception of Herbert and George Melville, the passengers seemed inclined to accept the offer.

"Come along, Melville," said the colonel; "you and your friend must join us."

"Please excuse me, colonel," answered Melville. "I would prefer not to drink."

"Oh, nonsense! To oblige me, now."

"Thank you; but I am traveling for my health, and it would not be prudent."

"Just as you say, Melville; but a little whisky would warm you up and do you good, in my opinion."

"Thank you all the same, colonel; but I think you must count me out."

The colonel shrugged his shoulders and beckoned Herbert.

"You can come, anyway; your health won't prevent."

Melville did not interfere, for he knew it would give offense, but he hoped his young clerk would refuse.

"Thank you," said Herbert; "I won't object to a glass of sarsaparilla."

"Sarsaparilla!" repeated the colonel, in amazement. "What's that?"

"We don't keep no medicine," growled the landlord.

"Have you root-beer?" asked Herbert.

"What do you take me for?" said the landlord, contemptuously. "I haven't got no root-beer. Whisky's good enough for any man."

"I hope you'll excuse me, then," said Herbert. "I am not used to any strong drinks."

"How old are you?" asked the colonel, rather contemptuously.

"Sixteen."

"Sixteen years old and don't drink whisky! My young friend, your education has been sadly neglected."

"I dare say it has," answered Herbert, good-naturedly.

"Gentlemen," said Col. Warner, apologetically, "the boy is a stranger, and isn't used to our free Western ways. He's got the makings of a man in him, and it won't be long before he'll get over his squeamishness, and walk up to the bar as quick as any one of us."

Herbert and Melville stood apart, while the rest of the company emptied their glasses, apparently at a gulp. It was clear that their refusal had caused them to be regarded with dislike and suspicion.

The accommodations of the Echo Gulch Hotel were far from luxurious. The chambers were scarcely larger than a small closet, clap-boarded but not plastered, and merely contained a bedstead. Washing accommodations were provided downstairs.

Herbert and George Melville were assigned to a single room, to which they would not have objected had the room been larger. It was of no use to indulge in open complaints, however, since others had to fare in the same way.

"This isn't luxury, Herbert," said Melville.

"No," answered the boy; "but I don't mind it if you don't."

"I am afraid I may keep you awake by my coughing, Herbert."

"Not if I once get to sleep. I sleep as sound as a top."

"I wish I did; but I am one of the wakeful kind. Being an invalid, I am more easily annoyed by small inconveniences. You, with your sturdy health, are more easily suited."

"Mr. Melville, I had just as lief sleep downstairs in a chair, and give you the whole of the bed."

"Not on my account, Herbert. I congratulate myself on having you for a roommate. If I had been traveling alone I might have been packed away with the colonel, who, by this time, would be even less desirable as a bedfellow than usual."

The worthy colonel had not been content with a single glass of whisky, but had followed it up several times, till his utterance had become thick, and his face glowed with a dull, brick-dust color.

Col. Warner had been assigned to the adjoining chamber, or closet, whichever it may be called. He did not retire early, however, while Herbert and George Melville did.

Strangely enough, Herbert, who was usually so good a sleeper, after a short nap woke up. He turned to look at his companion, for it was a moonlight night, and saw that he was sleeping quietly.

"I wonder what's got into me?" he thought; "I thought I should sleep till morning."

He tried to compose himself to sleep, but the more effort he made the broader awake he became. Sometimes it seems as if such unaccountable deviations from our ordinary habits were Heaven-sent. As Herbert lay awake he suddenly became aware of a conversation which was being carried on, in low tones, in the next room. The first voice he heard, he recognized as that of the colonel.

"Yes," he said, "some of the passengers have got money. There's that Stiefel probably carries a big sum in gold and notes. When I was speaking of the chance of the stage being robbed, he was uncommon nervous."

"Who's Stiefel?" was growled in another voice, which Herbert had no difficulty in recognizing as the landlord's.

"Oh, he's the fat, red-faced German. From his talk, I reckon he's come out to buy mines somewhere in Colorado."

"We'll save him the trouble."

"So we will—good joke, John. Oh, about this Stiefel, he carries his money in a belt round his waist. I infer that it is gold."

"Good! What about the others?"

"There's a tall, thin man—his name is Parker," proceeded the colonel; "he's smart, or thinks he is; you'll have to pull his stockings off to get his money. Ha, ha!"

"How did you find out, colonel?" asked the landlord, in admiration.

"Drew it out of him, sir. He didn't know who he was confiding in. He'll wonder how the deuce his hiding place was suspected."

Other passengers were referred to who have not been mentioned, and in each case the colonel was able to tell precisely where their money was kept.

"How about that milksop that wouldn't drink with us?" inquired the landlord, after a while.

"Melville? I couldn't find out where he keeps his cash. Probably he keeps it in his pocket. He doesn't look like a cautious man."

"Who's the boy?"

"Only a clerk or secretary of Melville's. He hasn't any money, and isn't worth attention."

"Very glad to hear it," thought Herbert. "I don't care to receive any attention from such gentry. But who would have thought the colonel was in league with stage robbers? I thought him a gentleman."

Herbert began to understand why it was that Col. Warner, if that was his real name, had drawn the conversation to stage robbers, and artfully managed to discover where each of the passengers kept his supply of money. It was clear that he was in league with the landlord of the Echo Gulch Hotel, who, it was altogether probable, intended to waylay the stage the next day.

This was a serious condition of affairs. The time had been when, in reading stories of adventure, Herbert had wished that he, too, might have some experience of the kind. Now that the opportunity had come, our hero was disposed to regard the matter with different eyes.

"What can be done," he asked himself, anxiously, "to escape the danger which threatens us to-morrow?"

CHAPTER XXIV. A MORNING WALK.

Herbert found it difficult to sleep from anxiety. He felt that the burden was too great for him alone to bear, and he desired to speak on the subject to George Melville. But there was a difficulty about doing this undetected, on account of the thinness of the partitions between the rooms. If he could hear Col. Warner, the latter would also be able to hear him.

The stage was to start at seven o'clock the next morning, and before that time some decision must be made. The first question was, should they, or should they not, take passage, as they had anticipated?

At half-past five, Herbert, turning in bed, found his bedfellow awake.

"Mr. Melville," he whispered, "I have something important to communicate, and cannot do so here on account of the danger of being heard in the next room. Are you willing to dress and take a little walk with me before breakfast?"

George Melville's physical condition did not make him usually favorable to early rising, but he knew Herbert well enough to understand that he had a satisfactory reason for his request.

"Yes, Herbert," he said, "I will get up."

Not a word was exchanged, for Mr. Melville's discretion prevailed over his curiosity. In ten minutes both were fully dressed and descended the stairs.

There was no one stirring except a woman, the landlord's wife, who was lighting the fire in order to prepare breakfast.

She regarded the two with surprise, and perhaps a little distrust.

"You're stirrin' early, strangers," she said.

"Yes," answered Melville, courteously, "we are going to take a little walk before breakfast; it may sharpen our appetites."

"Humph!" said the woman; "that's curious. I wouldn't get up so early if I wasn't obliged. There ain't much to see outdoors."

"It is a new part of the country to us," said Melville, "and we may not have another chance to see it."

"When will breakfast be ready?" asked Herbert.

"Half an hour, more or less," answered the woman, shortly.

"We will be back in time," he said.

The landlady evidently thought their early-rising a singular proceeding, but her suspicions were not aroused. She resumed her work, and Herbert and his friend walked out through the open door.

When they had reached a spot a dozen rods or more distant, Melville turned to his young clerk and asked:

"Well, Herbert, what is it?"

"I have discovered, Mr. Melville, that our stage is to be stopped to-day and the passengers plundered."

"How did you discover this?" asked Melville, startled.

"By a conversation which I overheard in the next chamber to us."

"But that chamber is occupied by Col. Warner."

"And he is one of the conspirators," said Herbert, quietly.

"Is it possible?" ejaculated Melville. "Can we have been so deceived in him? Does he propose to waylay the stage?"

"No, I presume he will be one of the passengers."

"Tell me all you know about this matter, Herbert. Who is engaged with him in this plot?"

"The landlord."

"I am not much surprised at this," said Melville, thoughtfully. "He is an ill-looking man, whose appearance fits the part of highwayman very well. Then you think the colonel is in league with him?"

"I am sure of that. Don't you remember how skillfully Col. Warner drew out of the passengers the hiding places of their money yesterday?"

"Yes."

"He has told all to the landlord, and he will no doubt make use of the knowledge. That is all, Mr. Melville. I could not rest till I had told you, so that you might decide what to do."

"It seems quite providential that you were kept awake last night, Herbert, otherwise this blow would have come upon us unprepared. Even with the knowledge that it impends, I hardly know what it is best for us to do."

"We might decide not to go in the stage," suggested Hebert.

"But we should have to go to-morrow. We cannot stay here, and there is no other way of traveling. As the colonel seems to think I have money, there would be another attack to-morrow. Besides, where could we stay except at this hotel, which is kept, as it appears, by the principal robber."

"That is true," said Herbert, puzzled; "I didn't think of that."

"I would quite as soon stand my chance of being robbed in the stage, as be attacked here. Besides, I cannot make up my mind to desert my fellow passengers. It seems cowardly to send them off to be plundered without giving them a hint of their danger."

"Couldn't we do that?"

"The result would be that they would not go, and there is no knowing how long we should be compelled to remain in this secluded spot."

"Mr. Melville," said Herbert, suddenly, "a thought has just struck me."

"I hope it may show us a way out of our danger."

"No, I am sorry to say that it won't do that."

"What is it, Herbert?"

"You remember that mention was made yesterday in the stage of a certain famous bandit named Jerry Lane?"

"Yes, I remember."

"Do you think it is possible that he and Col. Warner may be one and the same?"

"That is certainly a startling suggestion, Herbert. What reason have you for thinking so?"

"It was only a guess on my part; but you remember that the colonel said he was a man about his size."

"That might be."

"And he did not confine himself to the Western country, but might be met with in New York, or St. Louis. We met the colonel in Chicago."

"It may be as you surmise, Herbert," said George Melville, after a pause. "It did occur to me that our worthy landlord might be the famous outlaw in question, but the description to which you refer seems to fit the colonel better. There is one thing, however, that makes me a little incredulous."

"What is that, Mr. Melville?"

"This Jerry Lane I take to be cool and courageous, while the colonel appears to be more of a boaster. He looks like one who can talk better than he can act. If I had ever seen a description of his appearance, I could judge better."

The two had been walking slowly and thoughtfully, when they were startled by a rough voice.

"You're out early, strangers?"

Turning swiftly, they saw the dark, forbidding face of the landlord, who had approached them unobserved.

"Did he hear anything?" thought Herbert, anxiously.

"Yes, we are taking a little walk," said Melville, pleasantly.

"Breakfast will be ready soon. You'd better be back soon, if you're goin' by the stage this morning. You are goin', I reckon?" said the landlord, eyeing them sharply.

"We intend to do so," said Melville. "We will walk a little farther, and then return to the house."

The landlord turned and retraced his steps to the Echo Gulch Hotel.

"Do you think he heard anything that we were saying?" asked Herbert.

"I think not."

"I wonder what brought him out here?"

"Probably he wanted to make sure that we were going in the stage. He is laudably anxious to have as many victims and as much plunder as possible."

"You told him you were going in the stage?"

"Yes, I have decided to do so."

"Have you decided upon anything else, Mr. Melville?"

"Not positively; but there will be time to think of that. Did you hear where we were to be attacked?"

"At a point about five miles from here," said Herbert.

This he had gathered from the conversation he had overheard.

When the two friends reached the hotel, they found Col. Warner already downstairs.

"Good-morning, gentlemen!" he said. "So you have taken a walk? I never walk before breakfast, for my part."

"Nor do I often," said Melville. "In this case I was persuaded by my young friend. I am repaid by a good appetite."

"Can't I persuade you to try a glass of bitters, Mr. Melville?" asked the colonel.

"Thank you, colonel. You will have to excuse me."

"Breakfast's ready!" announced the landlady, and the stage passengers sat down at a long, unpainted, wooden table, where the food was of the plainest. In spite of the impending peril of which they, only, had knowledge, Herbert ate heartily, but Melville seemed preoccupied.

CHAPTER XXV. MELVILLE MAKES A SENSATION.

Col. Warner seemed in very good spirits. He ate and drank with violent enjoyment, and was as affable as usual. George Melville regarded him with curiosity.

"The man does not appear like a desperado or outlaw," he thought. "There is nothing to distinguish him from the majority of men one meets in ordinary intercourse. He is a problem to me, I should like to study him."

Col. Warner did not fail to observe the unconscious intentness with which Melville regarded him, and, for some reason, it did not please him.

"You have lost your appetite, Mr. Melville," he said, lightly. "You have been looking at me until—egad!—if I were a vain man, I should conclude there was something striking about my appearance."

"I won't gainsay that, Colonel," answered Melville, adroitly. "I confess I am not very hungry, and I will further confess that I have something on my mind."

"Indeed! Better make me your father confessor," said the colonel, whose suspicion or annoyance was removed by this ready reply.

"So I may, after a while," said Melville.

He took the hint, and ceased to regard the colonel.

The latter made himself generally social, and generally popular.

The stage drove round to the door after breakfast, and there was the usual bustle, as the passengers bestowed themselves inside.

George Melville had intended to watch narrowly the landlord and Col. Warner, to detect, if possible, the secret understanding which must exist between them. But he was deprived of an opportunity, for the very good reason that the landlord had disappeared, and was not again seen before their departure.

The driver gathered up his reins, cracked his whip, and the stage started. Herbert looked at George Melville a little anxiously, not knowing what course he had decided to take. They two, it will be remembered, were the only ones who knew of the intended attack.

Before the stage started, Melville quietly took the opportunity to hand his pocketbook to Herbert, saying, briefly: "It will be safer with you in case of an attack."

"But won't it be considered suspicious that you have no money about you?" suggested Herbert.

"I have a roll of bills in my pocket-fifty dollars," answered Melville.

They had no further opportunity of speaking, as one of the passengers came up where they were standing.

Herbert had already taken his seat in the coach, when his employer said: "Herbert, wouldn't you like to ride outside with the driver?"

"Yes, sir," answered Herbert, promptly, for he understood, that this was Mr. Melville's wish.

"It will give us more room, and you will have a better view."

"Yes, sir; I shall like it."

In a quick manner Herbert made the change, taking care not to look significantly at Melville, as some boys might have done, and thus excited suspicion.

For the first mile there was very little conversation.

Then Col. Warner spoke.

"Well, gentlemen," he said, "we are fairly on our way. Let us hope nothing will mar our pleasure."

"Do you anticipate anything?" asked George Melville.

"I! Why should I? We have a skillful driver, and I guarantee he won't tip us over."

"Mr. Melville was, perhaps, referring to the chance of the stage being stopped by some enterprising road agent," suggested Parker.

"Oho! Sits the wind in that quarter?" said the Colonel, laughing lightly. "Not the least chance of that—that is, the chance is very slight."

"You spoke differently yesterday," said the German capitalist.

"Did I? I didn't mean it, I assure you. We are as safe here as if we were riding in the interior of New York. I suppose I was only whiling away a few idle minutes."

"I am glad to hear it," said the German. "I shouldn't like to meet any of these gentlemen."

"Nor I," answered Melville; "but I am prepared to give him or them a warm reception."

As he spoke he drew a revolver from his pocket. He sat next to the door, and in an exposed situation.

"Put up your shooting iron, Mr. Melville," said Col. Warner, exhibiting a slight shade of annoyance. "Let me exchange places with you. I should prefer the post of danger, if' there is any."

"You are very kind, Colonel," said Melville, quietly, "but I don't care to change. I am quite satisfied with my seat."

"But, my dear sir, I insist—" said the Colonel, making a motion to rise.

"Keep your seat, Colonel! I insist upon staying where I am," answered Melville.

He was physically far from formidable, this young man, but there was a resolute ring in his voice that showed he was in earnest.

"Really, my dear sir," said the Colonel, trying to conceal his annoyance, "you have been quite misled by my foolish talk. I did not suppose you were so nervous."

"Possibly I may have a special reason for being so," returned George Melville.

"What do you mean?" demanded the Colonel, quickly. "If you have, we are all interested, and ought to know it."

"The Colonel is right," said the German. "If you know of any danger, it is only fair to inform us all."

"I am disposed to agree with you, gentlemen," said Melville. "Briefly, then, I have good reason to think that this company of passengers has been marked for plunder."

Col. Warner started, but, quickly recovering himself, he laughed uneasily.

"Tush!" he said, "I put no faith in it. Some one has been deceiving you, my friend."

But the other passengers took it more seriously.

"You evidently know something that we do not," said Parker.

"I do," answered Melville.

Col. Warner looked at him searchingly, but did not speak.

Now was the time to test George Melville's nerve. He was about to take a bold step.

"Gentlemen," he said, "I regret to say that I have every reason to believe there is a man in this stage who is in league with the road agents."

This statement naturally made a sensation.

There were seven passengers, and each regarded the rest with new-born suspicion. There seemed, on the whole, about as much reason to suspect one man as another, and each, with the exception of Melville, found himself looked upon with distrust.

"Pooh, Melville! You must have had bad dreams!" said Col. Warner, who was the first to recover his self-possession. "Really, I give you credit for a first-class sensation. As for you, gentlemen, you may take stock in this cock-and-bull story, if you like; I shall not. I, for one, have no fear of my fellow passengers. I regard them all as gentlemen, and shall not allow myself to be disturbed by any silly fears."

The air of calm composure with which the Colonel spoke served to tranquilize the rest of the passengers, who wished to put credit in his assurance.

"The Colonel speaks sensibly," said Mr. Parker, "and unless Mr. Melville assigns a reason for his remarkable belief, I am disposed to think we have taken alarm too quick."

"Of course, of course; all sensible men will think so," said the Colonel. "My friend, we shall be tempted to laugh at you if you insist on entertaining us with such hobgoblin fancies. My advice is, to put up that weapon of yours, and turn your attention to the scenery, which I can assure you, gentlemen, is well worthy of your admiration. Just observe the walls of yonder canyon, and the trees growing on the points."

"Gentlemen," said Melville, "I should be glad to take the view of the last speaker, if I had not positive proof that he is the man who has agreed to deliver us into the hands of a road agent within the space of half an I hour!"

"Sir, you shall answer for this!" exclaimed the Colonel, furiously, as he struggled to secure the weapon, his face livid with passion.

But two passengers, one the German, who, though short, was very powerful, forcibly prevented him.

CHAPTER XXVI. A COUNCIL OF WAR.

"Are you sure of what you say?" asked a passenger, turning with a puzzled look from George Melville, who, in the midst of the general excitement produced by his revelation, sat, not unmoved indeed, but comparatively calm. Courage and physical strength are by no means inseparable, and this frail young man, whose strength probably was not equal to Herbert's, was fearless in the face of peril which would daunt many a stalwart six-footer.

In reply to this very natural question, George Melville repeated the essential parts of the conversation which had taken place between Col. Warner and the landlord.

Col. Warner's countenance changed, and he inwardly execrated the imprudence that had made his secret plan known to one of the intended victims.

"Is this true, Col. Warner?" asked Parker.

"No, it's a lie!" returned the colonel, with an oath.

"Gentlemen!" said George Melville, calmly, "you can choose which you will believe. I will only suggest that this man managed very adroitly to find out where each one of us kept his money. You can also consider whether I have any cause to invent this story."

It was clear that the passengers were inclined to put faith in Melville's story.

"Gentlemen!" said the Colonel, angrily, "I never was so insulted in my life. I am a man of wealth, traveling on business; I am worth a quarter of a million at least. To associate me with road agents, whom I have as much reason to fear as you, is most ridiculous. This young man may be well-meaning, but he is under a most extraordinary hallucination. It is my belief that he dreamed the nonsense he has been retailing to you."

"Ask the driver to stop the stage," said Mr. Benson, a gentleman from Philadelphia. "If Mr. Melville's story is trustworthy, we may at any time reach the spot where the highwayman is lurking. We must have a general consultation, and decide what is to be done."

This proposal was approved, and the driver drew up the stage.

"I don't propose to remain in the company of men who so grossly misjudge me," said the Colonel, with dignity, as he made a motion to leave his fellow passengers.

"Stay here, sir!" said Mr. Benson, in a tone of authority. "We cannot spare you yet."

"Do you dare to detain me, sir?" exclaimed Warner, menacingly.

"Yes, we do," said the German. "Just stay where you are, Mr. Colonel, till we decide what to do."

As each one of the company had produced his revolver, the Colonel thought it prudent to obey.

"I am disgusted with this fooling," he said, "You're all a pack of cowards."

"Driver," said George Melville, "has this stage ever been robbed?"

"Several times," the driver admitted.

"When was the last time?"

"Two months since."

"Where did it happen?"

"About a mile further on."

"Did you ever see this gentleman before?" he asked, pointing to the colonel.

"Yes," answered the driver, reluctantly.

"When did he last ride with you?"

"On the day the stage was robbed," answered the driver.

The passengers exchanged glances, and then, as by a common impulse, all turned to Col. Warner, to see how he would take this damaging revelation. Disguise it as he might, he was clearly disconcerted.

"Is this true, colonel?" asked Benson.

"Yes, it is," answered Col. Warner, with some hesitation. "I was robbed, with the rest. I had four hundred dollars in my wallet, and the road agent made off with it."

"And yet you just now pooh-poohed the idea of a robbery, and said such things were gone by."

"I say so now," returned the colonel, sullenly. "I have a good deal of money with me, but I am willing to take my chances."

"Doubtless. Your money would be returned to you, in all probability, if, as we have reason to believe, you have a secret understanding with the thieves who infest this part of the country."

"Your words are insulting. Let go my arm, sir, or it will be the worse for you."

"Softly, softly, my good friend," said the German. "Have you any proposal to make, Mr. Melville?"

"Only this. Let us proceed on our journey, but let each man draw his revolver, and be ready to use it, if need be."

"What about the colonel?"

"He must go along with us. We cannot have him communicating with our enemies outside."

"Suppose I refuse, sir?"

"Then, my very good friend, I think we shall use a little force," said the German, carelessly pointing his weapon at the captive.

"I will go upon compulsion," said the colonel, "but I protest against this outrage. I am a wealthy capitalist from Chicago, who knows no more about road agents than you do. You have been deceived by this unsophisticated young man, who knows about as much of the world as a four-year-old child. It's a fine mare's nest he has found."

This sneer did not disturb the equanimity of George Melville.

"I should be glad to believe the colonel were as innocent as he claims," he said, "but his own words, overheard last night, contradict what he is now saying. When we have passed the spot indicated for the attack, we will release him, and give him the opportunity he seeks of leaving our company."

The passengers resumed their places in the stage, with the exception of Herbert, who again took his seat beside the driver. George Melville had not mentioned that it was Herbert, not himself, who had overheard the conversation between the colonel and the land lord, fearing to expose the boy to future risk.

Col. Warner sat sullenly between the German and Benson. He was evidently ill at ease and his restless glances showed that he was intent upon some plan of escape. Of this, however, such was the vigilance of his guards, there did not seem much chance.

The stage kept on its way till it entered a narrow roadway, lined on one side by a thick growth of trees.

Melville, watching the colonel narrowly, saw that, in spite of his attempt at calmness, his excitement was at fever heat.

The cause was very evident, for at this point a tall figure bounded from the underbrush, disguised by a black half mask, through which a pair of black eyes blazed fiercely.

"Stop the stage!" he thundered to the driver, "or I will put a bullet through your head."

The driver, as had been directed, instantly obeyed.

CHAPTER XXVII. COL. WARNER CHANGES FRONT.

It may seem a daring thing for one man to stop a stage full of passengers, and require them to surrender their money and valuables, but this has been done time and again in unsettled portions of the West. For the most part the stage passengers are taken by surprise, and the road agent is known to be a desperado, ready to murder in cold blood anyone who dares oppose him.

In the present instance, however, the passengers had been warned of their danger and were ready to meet it.

Brown—for, of course, the masked man was the landlord—saw four revolvers leveled at him from inside the stage.

"Let go that horse, my friend, or you are a dead man!" said Conrad Stiefel, calmly. "Two can play at your game."

Brown was taken by surprise, but he was destined to be still more astonished.

Col. Warner protruded his head from the window, saying:

"Yes, my friend, you had better give up your little plan. It won't work."

Such language from his confederate, on whom he fully relied, wholly disconcerted the masked robber.

"Well, I'll be blowed!" he muttered, staring, in ludicrous perplexity, at his fellow conspirator.

"Yes, my friend," said the colonel, "I shall really be under the necessity of shooting you myself if you don't leave us alone. We are all armed and resolute. I think you had better defer your little scheme."

Brown was not quick-witted. He did not see that his confederate was trying cunningly to avert suspicion from himself, and taking the only course that remained to him. Of course, he thought he was betrayed, and was, as a natural consequence, exasperated.

He released his hold on the horses, but, fixing his eyes on the colonel fiercely, muttered:

"Wait till I get a chance at you! I'll pay you for this."

"What an idiot!" thought Warner, shrugging his shoulders. "Why can't he see that I am forced to do as I am doing? I must make things plain to him."

He spoke a few words rapidly in Spanish, which Brown evidently understood. His face showed a dawning comprehension of the state of affairs, and he stood aside while the stage drove on.

"What did you say?" asked Conrad Stiefel, suspiciously.

"You heard me, sir," said the colonel, loftily. "You owe your rescue from this ruffian to me. Now, you can understand how much you have misjudged me."

Conrad Stiefel was not so easily satisfied of this.

"I heard what you said in Mexican, or whatever lingo it is, but I didn't understand it."

"Nor I," said Benson.

"Very well, gentlemen; I am ready to explain. I told this man that if he ever attempted to molest me I should shoot him in his track."

"Why didn't you speak to him in English?" asked Stiefel.

"Because I had a suspicion that the fellow was the same I met once in Mexico, and I spoke to him in Spanish to make sure. As he understood, I am convinced I was right."

"Who is it, then?" asked Benson.

"His name, sir, is Manuel de Cordova, a well-known Mexican bandit, who seems to have found his way to this neighborhood. He is a reckless desperado, and, though I addressed him boldly, I should be very sorry to meet him in a dark night."

This explanation was very fluently spoken, but probably no one present believed what the colonel said, or exonerated him from the charge which George Melville had made against him.

Five miles further on Col. Warner left the stage.

"Gentlemen," he said, "I am sorry to leave this pleasant company, but I have a mining claim in this neighborhood, and must bid you farewell. I trust that when you think of me hereafter, you will acquit me of the injurious charges which have been made against me. I take no credit to myself for driving away the ruffian who stopped us, but hope you won't forget it."

"No one interfered with the colonel when he proposed to leave the stage. Indeed, the passengers were unanimous in accepting his departure as a relief. In spite of his plausible representations, he was regarded with general suspicion.

"I wish I knew the meaning of that Spanish lingo," said the German, Conrad Stiefel.

"I can interpret it for you, Mr. Stiefel," said George Melville, quietly. "I have some knowledge of Spanish."

"What did he say?" asked more than one, eagerly.

"He said: 'You fool! Don't you see the plot has been discovered? It wasn't my fault. I will soon join you and explain.'"

This revelation made a sensation.

"Then he was in league with the road agent, after all?" said Parker.

"Certainly he was. Did you for a moment doubt it?" said Melville.

"I was staggered when I saw him order the rascal away."

"He is a shrewd villain!" said Benson. "I hope we shan't encounter him again."

CHAPTER XXVIII. THE CONSPIRATORS IN COUNCIL.

It is needless to say that Col. Warner's intention in leaving the stage was to join his fellow conspirator. There was no advantage in remaining longer with his fellow travelers, since the opportunity of plundering them had passed, and for the present was not likely to return. He had been a little apprehensive that they would try to detain him on suspicion, which would have been awkward, since they had numbers on their side, and all were armed. But in that unsettled country he would have been an elephant on their hands, and if the idea entered the minds of any one of the stage passengers, it was instantly dismissed.

When the stage was fairly on the way, Col. Warner went to a house where he was known, and asked for a horse.

"Any news, colonel?" asked the farmer, as he called himself. Really he was in league with the band of which Warner was the chief.

"No," answered the Colonel, gloomily. "No, worse luck! There might have been, but for an unfortunate circumstance."

"What's that?"

"There's plenty of good money in that stage coach and Brown and I meant to have it, but some sharp-eared rascal heard us arranging the details of the plan, and that spoiled it."

"Is it too late now?" asked the farmer, eagerly. "We can follow them, and overtake them yet, if you say so."

"And be shot for our pains. No, thank you. They are all on the alert, and all have their six-shooters in readiness. No, we must postpone our plan. There's one of the fellows that I mean to be revenged upon yet—the one that ferreted out our secret plan. I must bide my time, but I shall keep track of him."

Soon the Colonel, well-mounted, was on his way back to the rude inn where he had slept the night before.

Dismounting he entered without ceremony, and his eyes fell upon the landlord's wife, engaged in some household employment.

"Where's Brown?" he asked, abruptly.

"Somewheres round," was the reply.

"How long has he been home?"

"A matter of two hours. He came home awfully riled, but he wouldn't tell me what it was about. What's happened?"

"We've met with a disappointment—that's what's the matter."

"Did the passengers get the better of you?" asked the woman, for she was in her husband's guilty secrets, and knew quite well what manner of man she had married.

"They found out our little game," answered Warner, shortly, for he did not see any advantage in wasting words on his confederate's wife. "Which way did Brown go?"

"Yonder," answered Mrs. Brown, pointing in a particular direction.

Col. Warner tied his horse to a small sapling, and walked in the direction indicated.

He found the landlord sullenly reclining beneath a large tree.

"So you're back?" he said, surveying Warner with a lowering brow.

"Yes."

"And a pretty mess you've made of the job!" said the landlord, bitterly.

"It's as much your fault—nay, more!" said his superior, coolly.

"What do you mean?" demanded Brown, not over cordially.

"You would persist in discussing our plan last night in my room, though I warned you we might be overheard."

"Well?"

"We were overheard."

"What spy listened to our talk?"

"The young man, Melville—the one traveling with a boy. He kept it to himself till the stage was well on its way, and then he blabbed the whole thing to all in the stage."

"Did he mention you?"

"Yes, and you."

"Why didn't you tell him he lied, and shoot him on the spot?"

"Because I shouldn't have survived him five minutes," answered the colonel, coolly, "or, if I had, his companions would have lynched me."

Brown didn't look as if he would have been inconsolable had this occurred. In fact, he was ambitious to succeed to the place held by the colonel, as chief of a desperate gang of outlaws.

"I might have been dangling from a branch of a tree at this moment, had I followed your plan, my good friend Brown, and that would have been particularly uncomfortable."

"They might have shot me," said Brown, sullenly.

"I prevented that, and gave you timely warning. Of course it's a disappointment, but we shall have better luck next time."

"They've got away."

"Yes, but I propose to keep track of Melville and the boy, and have my revenge upon them in time. I don't care so much about the money, but they have foiled me, and they must suffer for it. Meanwhile, I want your help in another plan."

The two conferred together, and mutual confidence was re-established.

CHAPTER XXIX. A NEW HOME IN THE WOODS.

George Melville had no definite destination. He was traveling, not for pleasure, but for health, and his purpose was to select a residence in some high location, where the dry air would be favorable for his pulmonary difficulties.

A week later he had found a temporary home. One afternoon Herbert and he, each on horseback, for at that time public lines of travel were fewer than at present, came suddenly upon a neat, one-story cottage in the edge of the forest. It stood alone, but it was evidently the home of one who aimed to add something of the graces of civilization to the rudeness of frontier life.

They reined up simultaneously, and Melville, turning to Herbert, said: "There, Herbert, is my ideal of a residence. I should not be satisfied with a rude cabin. There I should find something of the comfort which we enjoy in New England."

"The situation is fine, too," said Herbert, looking about him admiringly.

The cottage stood on a knoll. On either side were tall and stately trees. A purling brook at the left rolled its silvery current down a gentle declivity, and in front, for half a mile, was open country.

"I have a great mind to call and inquire who lives here." said Melville. "Perhaps we can arrange to stay here all night."

"That is a good plan, Mr. Melville."

George Melville dismounted from his horse, and, approaching, tapped with the handle of his whip on the door.

"Who's there?" inquired a smothered voice, as of one rousing himself from sleep.

"A stranger, but a friend," answered Melville.

There was a sound as of some one moving, and a tall man, clad in a rough suit, came to the door, and looked inquiringly at Melville and his boy companion.

Though his attire was rude, his face was refined, and had the indefinable air of one who would be more at home in the city than in the country.

"Delighted to see you both," he said, cordially, offering his hand. "I don't live in a palace, and my servants are all absent, but if you will deign to become my guests I will do what I can for your comfort."

"You have anticipated my request," said Melville. "Let me introduce myself as George Melville, an invalid by profession, just come from New England in search of health. My young friend here is Herbert Carr, my private secretary and faithful companion, who has not yet found out what it is to be in poor-health. Without him I should hardly have dared to come so far alone."

"You are very welcome, Herbert," said the host, with pleasant familiarity. "Come in, both of you, and make yourselves at home."

The cottage contained two rooms. One was used as a bedchamber, the other as a sitting room. On the walls were a few pictures, and on a small bookcase against one side of the room were some twenty-five books. There was an easel and an unfinished picture in one corner, and a small collection of ordinary furniture.

"You are probably an artist," suggested Melville.

"Yes, you have hit it. I use both pen and pencil," and he mentioned a name known to Melville as that of a popular magazine writer.

I do not propose to give his real name, but we will know him as Robert Falkland.

"I am familiar with your name, Mr. Falkland," said Melville, "but I did not expect to find you here."

"Probably not," answered Falkland. "I left the haunts of civilization unexpectedly, some months ago, and even my publishers don't know where I am."

"In search of health?" queried Melville.

"Not exactly. I did, however, feel in need of a change. I had been running in a rut, and wanted to get out of it, so I left my lodgings in New York and bought a ticket to St. Louis; arrived there, I determined to come farther. So here I have been, living in communion with nature, seeing scarcely anybody, enjoying myself, on the whole, but sometimes longing to see a new face."

"And you have built this cottage?"

"No; I bought it of its former occupant, but have done something towards furnishing it; so that it has become characteristic of me and my tastes."

"How long have you lived here?"

"Three months; but my stay is drawing to a close."

"How is that?"

"Business that will not be put off calls me back to New York. In fact, I had appointed to-morrow for my departure."

Melville and Herbert exchanged a glance. It was evident that the same thought was in the mind of each.

"Mr. Falkland," said George Melville, "I have a proposal to make to you."

The artist eyed him in some surprise.

"Go on," he said.

"I will buy this cottage of you, if you are willing."

Falkland smiled.

"This seems providential," he said. "We artists and men of letters are apt to be short of money, and I confess I was pondering whether my credit was good with anybody for a hundred dollars to pay my expenses East. Once arrived there, there are plenty of publishers who will make me advances on future work."

"Then we can probably make a bargain," said Mr. Melville. "Please name your price."

Now, I do not propose to show my ignorance of real estate values in Colorado by naming the price which George Melville paid for his home in the wilderness. In fact, I do not know. I can only say that he gave Falkland a check for the amount on a Boston bank, and a hundred in cash besides.

"You are liberal, Mr. Melville," said Falkland, gratified. "I am afraid you are not a business man. I have not found that business men overpay."

"You are right, I am not a business man," answered Melville, "though I wish my health would admit of my being so. As to the extra hundred dollars, I think it worth that much to come upon so comfortable a home ready to my hand. It will really be a home, such as the log cabin I looked forward to could not be."

"Thank you," said Falkland; "I won't pretend that I am indifferent to money, for I can't afford to be. I earn considerable sums, but, unfortunately, I never could keep money, or provide for the future."

"I don't know how it would be with me," said Melville, "for I am one of those, fortunate or otherwise, who are born to a fortune. I have sometimes been sorry that I had not the incentive of poverty to induce me to work."

"Then, suppose we exchange lots," said the artist, lightly. "I shouldn't object to being wealthy."

"With all my heart," answered Melville. "Give me your health, your literary and artistic talent, and it is a bargain."

"I am afraid they are not transferable," said the artist, "but we won't prolong the discussion now. I am neglecting the rites of hospitality; I must prepare supper for my guests. You must know that here in the wilderness I am my own cook and dishwasher."

"Let me help you?" said Melville.

"No, Mr. Melville," said Herbert, "it is more in my line. I have often helped mother at home, and I don't believe you have had any experience."

"I confess I am a green hand," said Melville, laughing, "but, as Irish girls just imported say, 'I am very willing.'"

"On the whole, I think the boy can assist me better," said Falkland. "So, Mr. Melville, consider yourself an aristocratic visitor, while Herbert and myself, sons of toil, will minister to your necessities."

"By the way, where do you get your supplies?" asked Melville.

"Eight miles away there is a mining camp and store. I ride over there once a week or oftener, and bring home what I need."

"What is the name of the camp?"

"Deer Creek. I will point out to Herbert, before I leave you, the bridle path leading to it."

"Thank you. It will be a great advantage to us to know just how to live."

With Herbert's help an appetizing repast was prepared, of which all three partook with keen zest.

The next day Falkland took leave of them, and Melville and his boy companion were left to settle down in their new home.

CHAPTER XXX. A TERRIBLE MOMENT.

Melville's purchase comprised not only the cottage, but its contents, pictures and books included. This was fortunate, for though Herbert, who was strong, and fond of outdoor sports, such as hunting and fishing, could have contented himself, Melville was easily fatigued, and spent at least half of the day in the cabin. The books, most of which were new to him, were a great and unfailing resource.

Among the articles which Falkland left behind him were two guns, of which Herbert and Melville made frequent use. Herbert had a natural taste for hunting, though, at home, having no gun of his own, he had not been able to gratify his taste as much as he desired. Often after breakfast the two sallied forth, and wandered about in the neighboring woods, gun in hand. Generally Melville returned first, leaving Herbert, not yet fatigued, to continue the sport. In this way our hero acquired a skill and precision of aim which enabled him to make a very respectable figure even among old and practiced hunters.

One morning, after Melville had returned home, Herbert was led, by the ardor of the chase, to wander farther than usual. He was aware of this, but did not fear being lost, having a compass and knowing his bearings. All at once, as he was making his way along a wooded path, he was startled by hearing voices. He hurried forward, and the scene upon which he intruded was dramatic enough.

With arms folded, a white man, a hunter, apparently, stood erect, and facing him, at a distance of seventy-five or eighty feet, was an Indian, with gun raised, and leveled at the former.

"Why don't you shoot, you red rascal!" said the white man. "You've got the drop on me, I allow, and I am in your power."

The Indian laughed in his guttural way; but though he held the gun poised, he did not shoot. He was playing with his victim as a cat plays with a mouse before she kills it.

"Is white man afraid?" said the Indian, not tauntingly, but with real curiosity, for among Indians it is considered a great triumph if a warrior can inspire fear in his foe, and make him show the white feather.

"Afraid!" retorted the hunter. "Who should I be afraid of?"

"Of Indian."

"Don't flatter yourself, you pesky savage," returned the white man, coolly, ejecting a flood of tobacco juice from his mouth, for though he was a brave man, he had some drawbacks. "You needn't think I am afraid of you."

"Indian shoot!" suggested his enemy, watching the effect of this announcement.

"Well, shoot, then, and be done with it."

"White man no want to live?"

"Of course I want to live. Never saw a healthy white man that didn't. If I was goin' to die at all, I wouldn't like to die by the hands of a red rascal like you."

"Indian great warrior," said the dusky denizen of the woods, straightening up, and speaking complacently.

"Indian may be great warrior, but he is a horse thief, all the same," said the hunter, coolly.

"White man soon die, and Indian wear his scalp," remarked the Indian, in a manner likely to disturb the composure of even the bravest listener.

The hunter's face changed. It was impossible to reflect upon such a fate without a pang. Death was nothing to that final brutality.

"Ha! White man afraid now!" said the Indian, triumphantly—quick to observe the change of expression in his victim.

"No, I am not afraid," said the hunter, quickly recovering himself; "but it's enough to disgust any decent man to think that his scalp will soon be dangling from the belt of a filthy heathen like you. However, I suppose I won't know it after I'm dead. You have skulked and dogged my steps, you red hound, ever since I punished you for trying to steal my horse. I made one great mistake. Instead of beating you, I should have shot you, and rid the earth of you once for all."

"Indian no forget white man's blows. White man die, and Indian be revenged."

"Yes, I s'pose that's what it's coming to," said the hunter, in a tone of resignation. "I was a 'tarnal fool to come out this mornin' without my gun. If I had it you would sing a different song."

Again the Indian laughed, a low, guttural, unpleasant laugh, which Herbert listened to with a secret shudder. It was so full of malignity, and cunning triumph, and so suggestive of the fate which he reserved for his white foe, that it aggravated the latter, and made him impatient to have the blow fall, since it seemed to be inevitable.

"Why don't you shoot, you red savage?" he cried. "What are you waiting for?"

The Indian wished to gloat over the mental distress of his foe. He liked to prolong his own feeling of power—to enjoy the consciousness that, at any moment, he could put an end to the life of the man whom he hated for the blows which he felt had degraded him, and which he was resolved never to forget or forgive. It was the same feeling that has often led those of his race to torture their hapless victims, that they may, as long as possible, enjoy the spectacle of their agonies. For this reason he was in no hurry to speed on its way the fatal bullet.

Again the Indian laughed, and, taking aim, made a feint of firing, but withheld his shot. Pale and resolute his intended victim continued to face him. He thought that the fatal moment had come, and braced himself to meet his fate; but he was destined to be disappointed.

"How long is this goin' to last, you red hound?" he demanded. "If I've got to die, I am ready."

"Indian can wait!" said the savage, with a smile of enjoyment.

"You wouldn't find it prudent to wait if I were beside you," said the hunter. "It's easy enough to threaten an unarmed man. If some friend would happen along to foil you in your cowardly purpose——-"

"White man send for friend!" suggested the Indian, tauntingly.

Herbert had listened to this colloquy with varying emotions, and his anger and indignation were stirred by the cold-blooded cruelty of the savage. He stood motionless, seen by neither party, but he held his weapon leveled at the Indian, ready to shoot at an instant's warning. Brought up, as he had been, with a horror for scenes of violence, and a feeling that human life was sacred, he had a great repugnance to use his weapon, even where it seemed his urgent duty to do so. He felt that on him, young as he was, rested a weighty responsibility. He could save the life of a man of his own color, but only by killing or disabling a red man. Indian though he was, his life, too, was sacred; but when he threatened the life of another he forfeited his claim to consideration.

Herbert hesitated till he saw it was no longer safe to do so—till he saw that it was the unalterable determination of the Indian to kill the hunter, and then, his face pale and fixed, he pulled the trigger.

His bullet passed through the shoulder of the savage. The latter uttered a shrill cry of surprise and dismay, and his weapon fell at his feet, while he pressed his left hand to his wounded shoulder.

The hunter, amazed at the interruption, which had been of such essential service to him, lost not a moment in availing himself of it. He bounded forward, and before the savage well knew what he purposed, he had picked up his fallen weapon, and, leveling it at his wounded foe, fired.

His bullet was not meant to disable, but to kill. It penetrated the heart of the savage, and, staggering back, he fell, his face distorted with rage and disappointment.

"The tables are turned, my red friend!" said the hunter, coolly. "It's your life, not mine, this time!"

At that moment Herbert, pale and shocked, but relieved as well, pressed forward, and the hunter saw him for the first time.

"Was it you, boy, who fired the shot?" asked the hunter, in surprise.

"Yes," answered Herbert.

"Then I owe you my life, and that's a debt Jack Holden isn't likely to forget!"

CHAPTER XXXI. JACK HOLDEN ON THE INDIAN QUESTION.

It is a terrible thing to see a man stretched out in death who but a minute before stood full of life and strength. Herbert gazed at the dead Indian with a strange sensation of pity and relief, and could hardly realize that, but for his interposition, it would have been the hunter, not the Indian, who would have lost his life.

The hunter was more used to such scenes, and his calmness was unruffled.

"That's the end of the dog!" he said, touching with his foot the dead body.

"What made him want to kill you?" asked Herbert.

"Revenge," answered Holden.

"For what? Had you injured him?"

"That's the way he looked at it. One day I caught the varmint stealin' my best hoss. He'd have got away with him, too, if I hadn't come home just as I did. I might have shot him—most men would—but I hate to take a man's life for stealin'; and I took another way. My whip was lyin' handy, and I took it and lashed the rascal over his bare back a dozen times, and then told him to dust, or I'd serve him worse. He left, but there was an ugly look in his eyes, and I knew well enough he'd try to get even."

"How long ago was this?"

"Most a year. It's a long time, but an Indian never forgets an injury or an insult, and I knew that he was only bidin' his time. So I always went armed, and kept a good lookout. It was only this mornin' that he caught me at a disadvantage. I'd been taking a walk, and left my gun at home. He was prowlin' round, and soon saw how things stood. He'd have killed me sure, if you hadn't come in the nick of time."

"I am glad I was near," said Herbert, "but it seems to me a terrible thing to shoot a man. I'm glad it wasn't I that killed him."

"Mebbe it was better for me, as he was my enemy," said Jack Holden. "It won't trouble my conscience a mite. I don't look upon an Indian as a man."

"Why not?"

"He's a snake in the grass—a poisonous serpent, that's what I call him," said Jack Holden.

Herbert shook his head. He couldn't assent to this.

"You feel different, no doubt. You're a tenderfoot. You ain't used to the ways of these reptiles. You haven't seen what I have," answered Holden.

"What have you seen?" asked Herbert, judging correctly that Holden referred to some special experience.

"I'll tell you. You see, I'm an old settler in this Western country. I've traveled pretty much all over the region beyond the Rockies, and I've seen a good deal of the red men. I know their ways as well as any man. Well, I was trampin' once in Montany, when, one afternoon, I and my pard—he was prospectin'—came to a clearin', and there we saw a sight that made us all feel sick. It was the smokin' ruins of a log cabin, which them devils had set on fire. But that wasn't what I referred to. Alongside there lay six dead bodies—the man, his wife, two boys, somewhere near your age, a little girl, of maybe ten, and a baby—all butchered by them savages, layin'—in the hunter's vernacular—in their gore. It was easy to see how they'd killed the baby, by his broken skull. They had seized the poor thing by the feet, and swung him against the side of the house, dashin' out his brains."

Herbert shuddered, and felt sick, as the picture of the ruined home and the wretched family rose before his imagination.

"It was Indians that did it, of course," proceeded Holden. "They're born savage, and such things come natural to them."

"Are there no good Indians?" asked the boy.

"There may be," answered Jack Holden, doubtfully, "though I haven't seen many. They're as scarce as plums in a boardin' house puddin', I reckon."

I present this as Jack Holden's view, not mine. He had the prejudices of the frontier, and frontiersmen are severe judges of their Indian neighbors. They usually look at but one side of the picture, and are not apt to take into consideration the wrongs which the Indians have undeniably received. There is another extreme, however, and the sentimentalists who deplore Indian wrongs, and represent them as a brave, suffering and oppressed people, are quite as far away from a just view of the Indian question.

"What's your name, youngster?" asked Holden, with the curiosity natural under the circumstances.

"Herbert Carr."

"Do you live nigh here?"

Herbert indicated, as well as he could, the location of his home.

"I know—you live with Mr. Falkland. Are you his son?"

"No; Mr. Falkland has gone away."

"You're not living there alone, be you?"

"No; I came out here with a young man—Mr. Melville. He bought the cottage of Mr. Falkland, who was obliged to go East."

"You don't say so. Why, we're neighbors. I live three miles from here."

"Did you know Mr. Falkland?"

"Yes; we used to see each other now and then. He was a good fellow, but mighty queer. What's the use of settin' down and paintin' pictures? What's the good of it all?"

"Don't you admire pictures, Mr. Holden?" asked Herbert.

"That's that you called me? I didn't quite catch on to it."

"Mr. Holden. Isn't that your name?"

"Don't call me mister. I'm plain Jack Holden. Call me Jack."

"I will if you prefer it," said Herbert, dubiously.

"Of course I do. We don't go much on style in the woods. Won't you come home with me, and take a look at my cabin? I ain't used to company, but we can sit down and have a social smoke together, and then I'll manage to find something to eat."

"Thank you, Mr. Holden—I mean, Jack—but I must be getting home; Mr. Melville will be feeling anxious, for, as it is, I shall be late."

"Is Mr. Melville, as you call him, any way kin to you?"

"No; he is my friend and employer."

"Young man?"

"Yes; he is about twenty-five."

"How long have you two been out here?"

"Not much over a week."

"Why isn't Melville with you this morning?"

"He is in delicate health—consumption—and he gets tired sooner than I do."

"I must come over and see you, I reckon."

"I hope you will. We get lonely sometimes. If you would like to borrow something to read, Mr. Melville has plenty of books."

"Read!" repeated Jack. "No, thank you. I don't care much for books. A newspaper, now, is different. A man likes to know what's going on in the world; but I leave books to ministers, schoolmasters, and the like."

"If you don't read, how do you fill up your time, Jack?"

"My pipe's better than any book, lad. I'm goin' to set down and have a smoke now. Wish I had an extra pipe for you."

"Thank you," said Herbert, politely, "but I don't smoke."

"Don't smoke! How old are you?"

"Sixteen."

"Sixteen years old, and don't smoke! Why, where was you raised?"

"In the East," answered Herbert, smiling.

"Why, I smoked before I was three foot high, I was goin' to say. I couldn't get along without smokin'."

"Nor I without reading."

"Well, folks will have their different tastes, I allow. I reckon I'll be goin' back."

"Shan't you bury him?" asked Herbert, with a glance at the dead Indian.

"No; he wouldn't have buried me."

"But you won't leave him here? If you'll bury him, I'll help you."

"Not now, boy. Since you make a point of it, I'll come round to-morrow, and dig a hole to put him in. I'll take the liberty of carryin' home his shootin' iron. He won't need it where he's gone."

The two parted in a friendly manner, and Herbert turned his face homeward, grave and thoughtful.

CHAPTER XXXII. THE BLAZING STAR MINE.

Toward noon the next day George Melville and Herbert were resting from a country trip, sitting on a rude wooden settee which our hero had made of some superfluous boards, and placed directly in front of the house, when a figure was seen approaching with long strides from the shadow of the neighboring woods. It was not until he was close at hand that Herbert espied him.

"Why, it's Mr. Holden!" he exclaimed.

"Jack Holden, my lad," said the hunter, correcting him. "Is this the man you're living with?"

Jack Holden was unconventional, and had been brought up in a rude school so far as manners were concerned. It did not occur to him that his question might have been better framed.

"I am Mr. Melville," answered that gentleman, seeing that Herbert looked embarrassed. "Herbert is my constant and valued companion."

"He's a trump, that boy!" continued Holden. "Why, if it hadn't been for him, there'd been an end of Jack Holden yesterday."

"Herbert told me about it. It was indeed a tragic affair. The sacrifice of life is deplorable, but seemed to have been necessary, unless, indeed, you could have disabled him."

"Disabled him!" echoed the hunter. "That wouldn't have answered by a long shot. As soon as the reptile got well he'd have been on my trail ag'in. No, sir; it was my life or his, and I don't complain of the way things turned out."

"Have you buried him?" asked Herbert.

"Yes, I've shoved him under, and it's better than he deserved, the sneakin' rascal. I'm glad to make your acquaintance, Mr. Melville. Didn't know I had changed neighbors till the boy there told me yesterday. I've tramped over this mornin' to give you a call."

"You are very kind, Mr. Holden. Sit down here beside us."

"I'm more at home here," answered Holden, stretching himself on the ground, and laying his gun beside him. "How do you like Colorado?"

"Very much, as far as I have seen it," said Melville. "Herbert probably told you my object, in coming here?"

"He said you were ailin' some way."

"Yes, my lungs are weak. Since I have been here, I am feeling better and stronger, however."

"There don't seem to be anything the matter with the boy."

"Nothing but a healthy appetite," answered Herbert, smiling.

"That won't hurt anybody. Mr. Melville, do you smoke?"

"No, thank you."

"Queer! Don't see how you can do without it? Why, sir, I'd been homesick without my pipe. It's company, I tell you, when a chap's alone and got no one to speak to."

"I take it, Mr. Holden, you are not here for your health?"

"No, I should say not; I'm tough as a hickory nut. When I drop off it's more likely to be an Indian bullet than any disease. I'm forty-seven years old, and I don't know what it is to be sick."

"You are fortunate, Mr. Holden."

"I expect I am. But I haven't answered your question. I'm interested in mines, Mr. Melville. Have you ever been to Deer Creek?"

"Yes, I went over with Herbert to visit the store there one day last week."

"Did you ever hear of the Blazing Star Mine?"

"No, I believe not."

"I own it," said Holden. "It's a good mine, and would make me rich if I had a little more money to work it."

"Are the indications favorable, then?" asked Melville.

"It looks well, if that's what you mean. Yes, sir; the Star is a first-class property."

"Then it's a pity you don't work it."

"That's what I say myself. Mr. Melville, I've a proposal to make to you."

"What is it, Mr. Holden?"

"If you could manage to call me Jack, it would seem more social like."

"By all means, then, Jack!" said Melville smiling.

"You give me money enough to develop the mine, and I'll make half of it over to you."

"How much is needed?" asked Melville.

"Not over five hundred dollars. It's a bargain, I tell you."

"I do not myself wish to assume any business cares," said Melville.

Jack Holden looked disappointed.

"Just as you say," he responded.

"But Herbert may feel differently," continued Melville.

"I'd like the lad for a partner," said Holden, briskly.

"But I have no money!" said Herbert, in surprise.

George Melville smiled.

"If the mine is a good one," he said, "I will advance you the money necessary for the purchase of a half interest. If it pays you, you may become rich. Then you can repay the money."

"But suppose it doesn't, Mr. Melville," objected Herbert, "how can I ever repay you so large a sum?"

"On the whole, Herbert, I will take the risk."

"You are very kind, Mr. Melville," said Herbert, his face glowing with anticipation. To be half owner of a mine, with the chance of making a large sum of money, naturally elated him.

"Why shouldn't I be, Herbert? But I want to see the mine first."

"Can't you go over this afternoon?" asked Holden, eager to settle the matter as soon as possible.

"It is a long journey," said Melville, hesitating.

"You can stay overnight," said Jack Holden, "and come back in the morning."

"Very well; let us go then—that is, after dinner. Herbert, if you will set the table, we will see if we can't offer our friend here some refreshment. He is hungry, I am sure, after his long walk."

"You've hit it, Mr. Melville," said Holden. "I allow I'm as hungry as a wolf. But you don't set down to table, do you?"

"Oh, yes," answered Mr. Melville, smiling pleasantly.

"I ain't used to it," said Holden; "but I was once. Anyhow, it won't make no difference in the victuals."

When dinner was ready the three sat down, and did ample justice to it; but Jack Holden made such furious onslaughts that the other two could hardly keep pace with him. Fortunately, there was plenty of food, for Melville did not believe in economical housekeeping.

After dinner they set out for Deer Creek. As has been already explained, it was the name of a mining settlement. Now, by the way, it is a prosperous town, though the name has been changed. Then, however, everything was rude and primitive.

Jack Holden led the way to the Blazing Star Mine, and pointed out its capabilities and promise. He waited with some anxiety for Melville's decision.

"I don't understand matters very well," said Melville, "but I am willing to take a good deal on trust. If you desire it, I will buy half the mine, paying you five hundred dollars for that interest. That is, I buy it for Herbert."

"Hooray!" shouted Holden. "Give us your hand, pard. You are my partner now, you know."

As he spoke he gripped Herbert's hand in a pressure which was so strong as to be painful, and the necessary business was gone through.

So Herbert found himself a half owner of the Blazing Star Mine, of Deer Creek, Colorado.

"I hope your mine will turn out well, Herbert," said Melville, smiling.

"I wish it might for mother's sake!" said Herbert, seriously.

"It won't be my fault if it don't," said his partner. "I shall stay here now, and get to work."

"Ought I not to help you?" asked Herbert.

"No; Mr. Melville will want you. I will hire a man here to help me, and charge it to your share of the expenses."

So the matter was arranged; but Herbert rode over two or three times a week to look after his property.

CHAPTER XXXIII. GOOD NEWS FROM THE MINE.

"Well, Herbert, what news from the mine?" asked Melville, two weeks later, on Herbert's return from Deer Creek, whither he had gone alone.

"There are some rich developments, so Jack says. Do you know, Mr. Melville, he says the mine is richly worth five thousand dollars."

"Bravo, Herbert! That would make your half worth twenty-five hundred."

"Yes," said the boy complacently; "if we could sell at that figure, I could pay you back and have two thousand dollars of my own. Think of that, Mr. Melville," continued Herbert, his eyes glowing with pride and pleasure. "Shouldn't I be a rich boy?"

"You may do even better, Herbert. Don't be in a hurry to sell. That is my advice. If the present favorable indications continue, you may realize a considerably larger sum."

"So Jack says. He says he is bound to hold on, and hopes I will."

"You are in luck, Herbert."

"Yes, Mr. Melville, and I don't forget that it is to you I am indebted for this good fortune," said the boy, earnestly. "If you hadn't bought the property for me, I could not. I don't know but you ought to get some share ef the profits."

George Melville shook his head.

"My dear boy," he said, "I have more than my share of money already. Sometimes I feel ashamed when I compare my lot with others, and consider that for the money I have, I have done no work. The least I can do is to consider myself the Lord's trustee, and do good to others, when it falls in my way."

"I wish all rich men thought as you do, Mr. Melville; the world would be happier," said Herbert.

"True, Herbert. I hope and believe there is a considerable number who, like myself, feel under obligations to do good."

"I shall be very glad, on mother's account, if I can go home with money enough to make her independent of work. By the way, Mr. Melville, I found a letter from mother in the Deer Creek post office. Shall I read it to you?"

"If there is nothing private in it, Herbert."

"There is nothing private from you, Mr. Melville."

It may be explained that Deer Creek had already obtained such prominence that the post-office department had established an office there, and learning this, Herbert had requested his mother to address him at that place.

He drew the letter from his pocket and read it aloud.

We quote the essential portions.

"'I am very glad to hear that you have made the long journey in safety, and are now in health.'"

Herbert had not mentioned in his home letter the stage-coach adventure, for he knew that it would disturb his mother to think that he had been exposed to such a risk.

"It will do no good, you know," he said to Mr. Melville, and his friend had agreed with him.

"'It is very satisfactory to me,' continued Herbert, reading from the letter, 'that you are under the charge of Mr. Melville, who seems to me an excellent, conscientious young man, from whom you can learn only good.'"

"Your mother thinks very kindly of me," said Melville, evidently pleased.

"She is right, too, Mr. Melville," said Herbert, with emphasis.

"'It will no doubt be improving to you, my dear Herbert, to travel under such pleasant auspices, for a boy can learn from observation as well as from books. I miss you very much, but since the separation is for your advantage, I can submit to it cheerfully.

"'You ask me about my relations with Mr. Graham. I am still in the post office, and thus far nearly the whole work devolves upon me. Except in one respect, I am well treated. Mr. G-. is, as you know, very penurious, and grudges every cent that he has to pay out. When he paid me last Saturday night the small sum for which I agreed to assist him, he had much to say about his large expenses, fuel, lights, etc., and asked me if I wouldn't agree to work for two dollars a week, instead of three. I confess, I was almost struck dumb by such an exhibition of meanness, and told him that it would be quite impossible. Since then he has spent some of the time himself in the office, and asked me various questions about the proper way of preparing the mail, etc., and I think it is his intention, if possible, to get along without me. I don't know, if he absolutely insists upon it, but it would be better to accept the reduction than to give up altogether. Two dollars a week will count in my small household.'

"Did you ever hear of such meanness, Mr. Melville?" demanded Herbert, indignantly. "Here is Mr. Graham making, I am sure, two thousand dollars a year clear profit, and yet anxious to reduce mother from three to two dollars a week."

"It is certainly a very small business, Herbert. I think some men become meaner by indulgence of their defect."

"I shall write mother to give up the place sooner than submit to such a reduction. Three dollars a week is small enough in all conscience."

"I approve the advice, Herbert. If Mr. Graham were really cramped for money, and doing a poor business, it would be different. As it is, it seems to me he has no excuse for his extreme penuriousness."

"How pleasant it would be to pay a flying visit to Wayneboro," said Herbert, thoughtfully. "One never appreciates home until he has left it."

"That pleasure must be left for the future. It will keep."

"Very true, and when I do go home I want to go well fixed."

Herbert had already caught the popular Western phrase for a man well to do.

"We must depend on the Blazing Star Mine for that," said Melville, smiling. My young readers may like to know that, while Herbert was prospering financially, he did not neglect the cultivation of his mind. Among the books left by Mr. Falkland were a number of standard histories, some elementary books in French, including a dictionary, a treatise on natural philosophy, and a German grammar and reader.

"Do you know anything of French or German, Mr. Melville?" inquired our hero, when they made their first examination of the library.

"Yes, Herbert, I am a tolerable scholar in each."

"I wish I were."

"Would you like to study them?"

"Yes, very much."

"Then I will make you a proposal. You are likely to have considerable time at your disposal. If you will study either, or both, I will be your teacher."

"I should like nothing better," said Herbert, eagerly.

"Moreover, if you wish to study philosophy, I will aid you, though we are not in a position to illustrate the subject by experiments."

Herbert was a sensible boy. Moreover, he was fond of study, and he saw at once how advantageous this proposal was. He secured a private tutor for nothing, and, as he soon found, an excellent one. Though Mr. Melville had never been a teacher, he had an unusual aptitude for teaching, and it is hard to decide whether he or Herbert enjoyed more the hours which they now regularly passed in the relation of teacher and pupil.

It must be said, also, that while George Melville evinced an aptitude for teaching, Herbert showed an equal aptitude for learning. The tasks which he voluntarily undertook most boys would have found irksome, but he only found them a source of pleasure, and had the satisfaction, after a very short time, to find himself able to read ordinary French and German prose with comparative ease.

"I never had a better pupil," said George Melville.

"I believe I am the first you ever had," said Herbert, laughing.

"That is true. I spoke as if I were a veteran teacher."

"Then I won't be too much elated by the compliment."

CHAPTER XXXIV. TWO OLD ACQUAINTANCES REAPPEAR.

In the rude hotel kept by the outlaw, whom we have introduced under the name of Brown, there sat two men, to neither of whom will my readers need an introduction. They have already appeared in our story.

One was Brown himself, the other Col. Warner, or, as we may as well confess, Jerry Lane, known throughout the West as an unscrupulous robber and chief of a band of road agents, whose depredations had been characterized by audacity and success.

Brown was ostensibly an innkeeper, but this business, honest enough in itself, only veiled the man's real trade, in which he defied alike the laws of honesty and of his country. The other was by turns a gentleman of property, a merchant, a cattle owner, or a speculator, in all of which characters he acted excellently, and succeeded in making the acquaintance of men whom he designed to rob.

The two men wore a sober look. In their business, as in those more legitimate, there are good times and dull times, and of late they had not succeeded.

"I want some money, captain," said Brown, sullenly, laying down a black pipe, which he had been smoking.

"So do I, Brown," answered Warner, as we will continue to call him. "It's a dry time with me."

"You don't understand me, captain," continued Brown. "I want you to give me some money."

"First you must tell me where I am to get it," answered Warner, with a shrug of his shoulders.

"Do you mean to say you have no money?" asked Brown, frowning.

"How should I have?"

"Because in all our enterprises you have taken the lion's share, though you haven't always done the chief part. You can't have spent the whole."

"No, not quite; but I have nothing to spare. I need to travel about, and—"

"You've got a soft thing," grumbled Brown. "You go round and have a good time while I am tied down to this fourth-rate tavern in the woods."

"Well, it isn't much more than that," said Warner, musingly.

"Do you expect me to keep a first-class hotel?" demanded Brown, defiantly.

"No, of course not. Brown," continued Warner, soothingly, "don't let us quarrel; we can't afford it. Let us talk together reasonably."

"What have you to say?"

"This, that it isn't my fault if things have gone wrong. Was it my fault that we found so little cash in that last store we broke open?"

"Nineteen dollars!" muttered Brown, contemptuously.

"Nineteen dollars, as you say. It didn't pay us for our trouble. Well, I was as sorry as you. I fail to see how it was my fault. Better luck next time."

"When is the next time to be?" asked Brown, somewhat placated.

"As soon as you please."

"What is it?"

"I will tell you. You remember that stagecoach full of passengers that fooled us some time since?"

"I ought to."

"I always meant to get on the track of that Melville, who spoiled our plot by overhearing us and giving us away to the passengers. He is very rich, so the boy who was with him told me, and I have every reason to rely upon his statement. Well, I want to be revenged upon him, and, at the same time, to relieve him of the doubtless large sum of money which he keeps with him."

"I'm with you. Where is he?"

"I have only recently ascertained—no matter how. He lives in a small cabin, far from any other, about eight miles from the mining town of Deer Creek."

"I know the place."

"Precisely. No one lives there with him except the boy, and it would be easy enough to rob him. I saw a man from Deer Creek yesterday. He tells me that Melville has bought for the boy a half share in a rich mine, and is thought to have at least five thousand dollars in gold and bills in his cabin."

Brown's eyes glistened with cupidity.

"That would be a big haul," he said.

"Of course, it would. Now, Brown, while you have been grumbling at me I have been saving this little affair for our benefit—yours and mine. We won't let any of the rest of them into it, but whatever we find we will divide, and share alike."

"Do you mean this, captain?"

"Yes, I mean it, friend Brown. You shan't charge me with taking the lion's share in this case. If there are five thousand dollars, as my informant seems to think, your share shall be half."

"Twenty-five hundred dollars!"

"Exactly; twenty-five hundred dollars."

"That will pay for my hard luck lately," said Brown, his face clearing.

"Very handsomely, too."

"When shall we start?"

"To-morrow morning. We will set out early in the morning; and, by the way, Brown, it's just as well not to let your wife or anyone else know where we are going."

"All right," answered Brown, cheerfully.

The next morning the two worthies set out their far from meritorious errand. Brown told his wife vaguely, in reply to her questioning, that he was called away for a few days on business.

If he expected to evade further question by this answer, he was mistaken. Mrs. Brown was naturally of a jealous and suspicious temperament, and doubt was excited in her breast.

"Where shall I say you have gone if I am asked?" she said.

"You may say that you don't know," answered Brown, brusquely.

"I don't think much of a man who keeps secrets from his wife," said Mrs. Brown, coldly.

"And I don't think much of a man who tells everything to his wife," retorted Brown. "It's all right, Kitty, You needn't concern yourself. But the captain and I are on an expedition, which, to be successful, needs to be kept secret."

Mrs. Brown was not more than half convinced, but she was compelled to accept this statement, for her husband would vouchsafe no other.

That part of the State into which they journeyed was not new ground to either. They were familiar with all the settled portion of Colorado, and had no difficulty in finding the cabin occupied by George Melville.

Now it happened that they reached the modest dwelling in the woods about three o'clock in the afternoon. Herbert had ridden over to Deer Creek to look after his mining property, and it was not yet time to expect him back. George Melville was therefore left alone.

Knowing, as my young readers do, his literary tastes, they will understand that, though left alone, he was not lonely. The stock of books which he had bought from his predecessor was to him an unfailing resource. Moreover, he had taken up Italian, of which he knew a little, and was reading in the original the "Divina Comedia" of Dante, a work which consumed many hours, and was not likely soon to be over. To-day, however, for some reason Melville found it more difficult than usual to fix his mind upon his pleasant study. Was it a presentiment of coming evil that made him so unusually restless? At all events, the hours, which were wont to be fleet-footed, passed with unusual slowness, and he found himself longing for the return of his young friend.

"I don't know what has got into me to-day," said Melville to himself. "It's only three o'clock, yet the day seems very long. I wish Herbert would return. I feel uneasy. I don't know why. I hope it is not a presage of misfortune. I shall not be sure that something has not happened to Herbert till I see him again."

As he spoke George Melville rose from his chair, and was about to put on his hat and take a short walk in the neighboring woods, when he heard the tramp of approaching horses. Looking out from the window, he saw two horsemen close at hand.

He started in dismay, for in the two men he was at no loss in recognizing his stagecoach companion, Col. Warner, and the landlord who had essayed the part of a road agent.

CHAPTER XXXV. MELVILLE IN PERIL.

Col. Warner and his companion enjoyed the effect of their presence upon their intended victim, and smiled in a manner that boded little good to Melville, as they dismounted from their steeds and advanced to the door of the cabin.

"How are you, Melville?" said Warner, ironically. "I see you have not forgotten me."

"No, I have not forgotten you," answered Melville, regarding his visitor uneasily.

"This is my friend, Mr. Brown. Perhaps you remember him?"

"I do remember him, and the circumstances under which I last saw him," replied Melville, rather imprudently.

Brown frowned, but he did not speak. He generally left his companion to do the talking.

"Being in the neighborhood, we thought we'd call upon you," continued Col. Warner.

"Walk in, gentlemen, if you see fit," said Melville. "I suppose it would be only polite to say that I am glad to see you, but I have some regard for truth, and cannot say it."

"I admire your candor, Mr. Melville. Walk in, Brown. Ha! upon my word, you have a nice home here. Didn't expect to see anything of the kind in this wilderness. Books and pictures! Really, now, Brown, I am quite tempted to ask our friend, Melville, to entertain us for a few days."

"I don't think it would suit you," said Melville, dryly. "You are probably more fond of exciting adventure than of books."

"Does the boy live with you?" asked Warner, dropping his bantering tone, and looking about his searchingly.

"Yes, he is still with me."

"I don't see him."

"Because he has gone to Deer Creek on business."

When Melville saw the rapid glance of satisfaction interchanged by the two visitors he realized that he had made an imprudent admission. He suspected that their design was to rob him, and he had voluntarily assured them that he was alone, and that they could proceed without interruption.

"Sorry not to see him," said Warner. "I'd like to renew our pleasant acquaintance."

Melville was about to reply that Herbert would be back directly, when it occurred to him that this would be a fresh piece of imprudence. It would doubtless lead them to proceed at once to the object of their visit, while if he could only keep them till his boy companion did actually return, they would at least be two to two. Even then they would be by no means equally matched, but something might occur to help them.

"I suppose Herbert will return by evening," he replied. "You can see him if you remain till then."

Another expression of satisfaction appeared upon the faces of his two visitors, but for this he was prepared.

"Sorry we can't stay till then," said Warner, "but business of importance will limit our stay. Eh, Brown?"

"I don't see the use of delaying at all!" growled Brown, who was not as partial as his companion to the feline amusement of playing with his intended victim.

With him, on the contrary, it was a word, and a blow, and sometimes the blow came first.

"Come to business!" continued Brown, impatiently, addressing his associate.

"That is my purpose, friend Brown."

"Mr. Melville, it is not solely the pleasure of seeing you that has led my friend and myself to call this afternoon."

Melville nodded.

"So I supposed," he said.

"There is a little unfinished business between us, as you will remember. I owe you a return for the manner in which you saw fit to throw suspicion upon me some time since, when we were traveling together."

"I shall be very glad to have you convince me that I did you an injustice," said Melville. "I was led to believe that you and your friend now present were leagued together to rob us of our money and valuables. If it was not so—"

"You were not very far from right, Mr. Melville. Still it was not polite to express your suspicions so rudely. Besides, you were instrumental in defeating our plan."

"I can't express any regret for that, Col. Warner, or Jerry Lane, as I suppose that is your real name."

"I am Jerry Lane!" said Warner, proudly. "I may as well confess it, since it is well that you should know with whom you have to deal. When I say that I am Jerry Lane, you will understand that I mean business."

"I do," answered Melville, quietly.

"You know me by reputation?" said the outlaw, with a curious pride in his unenviable notoriety.

"I do."

"What do men say of me?"

"That you are at the head of a gang of reckless assassins and outlaws, and that you have been implicated in scores of robberies and atrocities."

This was not so satisfactory.

"Young man," said Lane—to drop his false name—"I advise you to be careful how you talk. It may be the worse for you. Now, to come to business, how much money have you in the house?"

"Why do you ask, and by what right?"

"We propose to take it. Now answer my question."

"Gentlemen, you will be very poorly paid for the trouble you have taken in visiting me. I have very little money."

"Of course, you say so. We want an answer."

"As well as I can remember I have between forty and fifty dollars in my pocketbook."

Brown uttered an oath under his breath, and Lane looked uneasy.

"That's a lie!" said Brown, speaking first. "We were told you had five thousand dollars here."

"Your informant was badly mistaken, then. I am not very wise, perhaps, in worldly matters, but I certainly am not such a fool as to keep so large a sum of money in a lonely cabin like this."

"Perhaps not so much as that," returned Lane. "I don't pretend to say how much you have. That is for you to tell us."

George Melville drew from his pocket a wallet, and passed it to the outlaw.

"Count the money for yourself, if you wish," he said. "You can verify my statement."

Lane opened the wallet with avidity, and drew out the contents. It was apparent at the first glance that the sum it contained was small. It was counted, however, and proved to amount to forty-seven dollars and a few silver coins.

The two robbers looked at each other in dismay. Was it possible that this was all? If so, they would certainly be very poorly paid for their trouble.

"Do you expect us to believe, Mr. Melville," said Jerry Lane, sternly, "that this is all the money you have?"

"In this cabin—yes."

"We are not so easily fooled. It is probably all you carry about with you; but you have more concealed somewhere about the premises. It will be best for you to produce at once, unless you are ready to pass in your checks."

"That means," said Melville, growing pale in spite of himself, for he knew from report the desperate character of his guests, "that means, I suppose, that you will kill me unless I satisfy your rapacity."

"It does," said Lane, curtly. "Now for your answer!"

"Gentlemen, I cannot accomplish impossibilities. It is as I say. The money in your hands is all that I have by me."

"Do you mean to deny that you are rich?" asked Lane.

"No, I do not deny it. That is not the point in question. You ask me to produce all the money I have with me. I have done so."

"Do you believe this, Brown?" asked the captain, turning to his subordinate.

"No, I don't."

"It is strictly true."

"Then," said Brown, "you deserve to die for having no more money for us."

"True," chimed in Lane. "Once more, will you produce your secret hoard?"

"I have none."

"Then you must be dealt with in the usual way. Brown, have you a rope?"

"Yes."

"Is there a convenient tree near by."

"We'll find one."

The two seized Melville, and, despite his resistance, dragged him violently from the cabin, and adjusted a rope about his neck. The young man was pale, and gave himself up for lost.

CHAPTER XXXVI. THE MINE IS SOLD.

While his friend was in peril, where was Herbert?

For him, too, it had been an exciting day—Deer Creek had been excited by the arrival of a capitalist from New York, whose avowed errand it was to buy a mine. Reports from Deer Creek had turned his steps thither, and all the mine owners were on the qui vive to attract the attention of the monied man. It was understood that he intended to capitalize the mine, when purchased, start a company, and work it by the new and improved methods, which had replaced the older and ruder appliances at first employed.

Mr. Compton, though not a mining expert, was a shrewd man, who weighed carefully the representations that were made to him, and reserved his opinion. It was clear that he was not a man who would readily be taken in, though there were not wanting men at Deer Creek who were ready to palm off upon him poor or worthless mines. About the only mine owners who did not seek him were the owners of the Blazing Star, both of whom were on the ground. The mine was looking up. The most recent developments were the most favorable, and the prospects were excellent. They might, indeed, "peter out" as the expression is, but it did not seem likely.

"Jack," said Herbert, "shall we invite Mr. Compton to visit our mine?"

"No," answered Jack Holden; "I am willing to keep it."

"Wouldn't you sell?"

"Yes, if I could get my price."

"What is your price?"

"Twenty-five thousand dollars for the whole mine!"

"That is twelve thousand five hundred for mine," said Herbert, his cheek flushing with the excitement he felt.

"You've figured it out right, my lad," said his partner.

"That would leave me twelve thousand after I have paid up Mr. Melville for the sum I paid in the beginning."

"Right again, my lad."

"Why, Jack!" exclaimed Herbert. "Do you know what that means? It means that I should be rich—that my mother could move into a nicer house, that we could live at ease for the rest of our lives."

"Would twelve thousand dollars do all that?"

"No; but it would give me a fund that would establish me in business, and relieve me of all anxiety. Jack, it's too bright to be real."

"We may not be able to sell the mine at that figure, Herbert. Don't let us count our chickens before they are hatched, or we may be disappointed. I'm as willin' to keep the mine as to sell it."

"Jack, here is Mr. Compton coming," said Herbert.

The capitalist paused, and addressing Herbert, said:

"Have you anything to do with the mine, my lad?"

"I am half owner," answered Herbert, promptly, and not without pride.

"Who is the other half owner?"

"Mr. Holden," answered Herbert, pointing out Jack.

"May I examine the mine?"

"You are quite welcome to, sir."

Possibly the fact that this mine alone had not been pressed upon him for purchase, predisposed Mr. Compton to regard it with favor. Every facility was offered him, and Jack Holden, who thoroughly understood his business, gave him the necessary explanations.

After an hour spent in the examination, Mr. Compton came to business.

"Is the mine for sale?" he asked.

"Yes, sir."

"What is your price?"

"Twenty-five thousand dollars."

"Is that your lowest price?"

"It is."

Jack Holden wasted no words in praising the mine, and this produced a favorable impression on the capitalist with whom he was dealing.

"I'll take it," he answered.

"Then it's a bargain."

Herbert found it difficult to realize that these few words had made him a rich boy. He remained silent, but in his heart he was deeply thankful, not so much for himself, as because he knew that he was now able to rejoice his mother's heart, and relieve her from all pecuniary cares or anxieties.

"You've made a good bargain, sir, if I do say it," said Jack Holden. "For my own part, I wasn't so particular about selling the mine, but my young partner here is differently placed, and the money will come handy to him."

"You are rather young for a mine owner," said Mr. Compton, regarding Herbert with some curiosity.

"Yes, sir; I believe I am the youngest mine owner here."

"Are you a resident of this State?"

"Only temporarily, sir. I came here with a friend whose lungs are weak."

"You expect to return to the East soon?"

"Yes, sir."

"When you do, come to see me. I am a commission merchant in Boston. If it is your intention to follow a business life, I may be able to find you a place."

"Thank you, sir; I should like nothing better."

"To-morrow," said Mr. Compton, "I will come here and complete the purchase."

"Jack," said Herbert, when the new purchaser of the mine had left them, "there is no work for us here. Come with me, and let us together tell Mr. Melville the good news."

"A good thought, my lad!"

So the two mounted their horses, and left Deer Creek behind them. They little suspected how sorely they were needed.

CHAPTER XXXVII. TO THE RESCUE.

Herbert and his companion drew near the forest cabin, which had been the home of the former, without a suspicion that George Melville was in such dire peril. The boy was, indeed, thinking of him, but it was rather of the satisfaction his employer would feel at his good fortune.

"Somehow I feel in a great hurry to get there, Jack," said Herbert. "I shall enjoy telling Mr. Melville of my good luck."

"He's a fine chap, that Melville," said Jack Holden, meaning no disrespect by this unceremonious fashion of speech.

"That he is! He's the best friend I ever had, Jack," returned Herbert, warmly.

"It's a pity he's ailing."

"Oh, he's much stronger than he was when he came out here. All the unfavorable symptoms have disappeared."

"Maybe he'll outgrow it. I had an uncle that was given up to die of consumption, when he was about Melville's age, and he died only last year at the age of seventy-five."

"That must have been slow consumption, Jack," said Herbert, smiling. "If Mr. Melville can live as long as that, I think neither he nor his friends will have reason to complain."

"Is he so rich, lad?"

"I don't know how rich, but I know he has plenty of money. How much power a rich man has," said Herbert, musingly. "Now, Mr. Melville has changed my whole life for me. When I first met him I was working for three dollars a week. Now I am worth twelve thousand dollars!"

Herbert repeated this with a beaming face. The good news had not lost the freshness of novelty. There was so much that he could do now that he was comparatively rich. To do Herbert justice, it was not of himself principally that he thought. It was sweet to reflect that he could bring peace, and joy, and independence to his mother. After all, it is the happiness we confer that brings us the truest enjoyment. The selfish man who eats and drinks and lodges like a prince, but is unwilling to share his abundance with others, knows not what he loses. Even boys and girls may try the experiment for themselves, for one does not need to be rich to give pleasure to others.

"Come, Jack, let us ride faster; I am in a hurry," said Herbert, when they were perhaps a quarter of a mile distant from the cabin.

They emerged from the forest, and could now see the cottage and its surroundings. They saw something that almost paralyzed them.

George Melville, with a rope round his neck, stood beneath a tree. Col. Warner was up in the tree swinging the rope over a branch, while Brown, big, burly and brutal, pinioned the helpless young man in his strong arms.

"Good heavens! Do you see that?" exclaimed Herbert. "It is the road agents. Quick, or we shall be too late!"

Jack had seen. He had not only seen, but he had already acted. Quick as thought he raised his weapon, and covered Brown. There was a sharp report, and the burly ruffian fell, his heart pierced by the unerring bullet.

Herbert dashed forward, and, seizing the rope, released his friend.

"Thank Heaven, Herbert! You have saved my life!" murmured Melville, in tones of heartfelt gratitude.

"There's another of them!" exclaimed Jack Holden, looking up into the tree, and he raised his gun once more.

"Don't shoot!" exclaimed the man, whom we know best as Col. Warner; "I'll come down."

So he did, but not in the manner he expected. In his flurry, for he was not a brave man, outlaw though he was, he lost his hold and fell at the feet of Holden.

"What shall we do with him, Mr. Melville?" asked Jack. "He deserves to die."

"Don't kill him! Bind him, and give him up to the authorities."

"I hate to let him off so easy," said Jack, but he did as Melville wished. But the colonel had a short reprieve. On his way to jail, a bullet from some unknown assailant pierced his temple, and Jerry Lane, the notorious road agent, died, as he had lived, by violence.

CHAPTER XXXVIII. CONCLUSION.

It had been the intention of George Melville to remain in Colorado all winter, but his improved health, and the tragic event which I have just narrated, conspired to change his determination.

"Herbert," he said, when the business connected with the sale of the mine had been completed, "how would you like to go home?"

"With you?"

"Yes, you don't suppose I would remain here alone?"

"If you feel well enough, Mr. Melville, there is nothing I should like better."

"I do feel well enough. If I find any unfavorable symptoms coming back, I can travel again, but I am anxious to get away from this place, where I have come so near losing my life at the hands of the outlaws."

There was little need of delay. Their preparations were soon made. There was an embarrassment about the cottage, but that was soon removed.

"I'll buy it of you, Mr. Melville," said Jack Holden.

"I can't sell it to you, Mr. Holden."

"I will give you a fair price."

"You don't understand me," said George Melville, smiling. "I will not sell it, because I prefer to give it."

"Thank you, Mr Melville, but you know I am not exactly a poor man. The sale of the mine——"

"Jack," said Melville, with emotion, "would you have me forget that it is to you and Herbert that I owe my rescue from a violent and ignominious death?"

"I want no pay for that, Mr. Melville."

"No, I am sure you don't. But you will accept the cabin, not as pay, but as a mark of my esteem."

Upon that ground Jack accepted the cottage with pleasure. Herbert tried to tempt him to make a visit to the East, but he was already in treaty for another mine, and would not go.

The two stayed a day in Chicago on their way to Boston.

"I wonder if Eben is still here?" thought Herbert.

He soon had his question answered. In passing through a suburban portion of the great city, he saw a young man sawing wood in front of a mean dwelling, while a stout negro was standing near, with his hands in his pockets, surveying the job. He was the proprietor of a colored restaurant, and Eben was working for him.

Alas, for Eben! The once spruce dry-goods clerk was now a miserable-looking tramp, so far as outward appearances went. His clothes were not only ragged, but soiled, and the spruce city acquaintances whom he once knew would have passed him without recognition.

"Eben!"

Eben turned swiftly as he heard his name called, and a flush of shame overspread his face.

"Is it you, Herbert?" he asked, faintly.

"Yes, Eben. You don't seem very prosperous."

"I never thought I should sink so low," answered Eben, mournfully, "as to saw wood for a colored man."

"What are you talkin' about?" interrupted his boss, angrily. "Ain't I as good as a worfless white man that begged a meal of vittles of me, coz he was starvin'?

You jest shut up your mouf, and go to work."

Eben sadly resumed his labor. Herbert pitied him, in spite of his folly and wickedness.

"Eben, do you owe this man anything?" he added.

"Yes, he does. He owes me for his dinner. Don't you go to interfere!" returned the colored man.

"How much was your dinner worth?" asked Herbert, putting his hand into his pocket.

"It was wuf a quarter."

"There is your money! Now, Eben, come with me."

"I've been very unfortunate," wailed Eben.

"Would you like to go back to Wayneboro?" asked Herbert.

"Yes, anywhere," answered Eben, eagerly. "I can't make a livin' here. I have almost starved sometimes."

"Eben, I'll make a bargain with you. If I will take you home, will you turn over a new leaf, and try to lead a regular and industrious life?"

"Yes, I'll do it," answered Eben.

"Then I'll take you with me to-morrow."

"I shouldn't like my old friends to see me in these rags," said Eben, glancing with shame at his tattered clothes.

"They shall not. Come with me, and I will rig you out anew."

"You're a good fellow, Herbert," said Eben, gratefully. "I'm sorry for the way I treated you."

"Then it's all right," said Herbert. Herbert kept his promise. He took Eben to a barber shop, where there were also baths, having previously purchased him a complete outfit, and Eben emerged looking once more like the spruce dry-goods salesman of yore.

One day not long afterwards Mrs. Carr was sitting in her little sitting room, sewing. She had plenty of leisure for this work now, for Mr. Graham had undertaken to attend to the post-office duties himself. It was natural that she should think of her absent boy, from whom she had not heard for a long time.

"When shall I see him again?" she thought, wearily.

There was a knock at the outer door.

She rose to open it, but, before she could reach it, it flew open, and her boy, taller and handsomer than ever, was in her arms.

"Oh, Herbert!"

It was all she could say, but the tone was full of joy.

"How I have missed you!"

"We will be together now, mother."

"I hope so, Herbert. Perhaps you can find something to do in Wayneboro, and even if it doesn't pay as well—"

"Mother," interrupted Herbert, laughing, "is that the way to speak to a rich boy like me?"

"Rich?"

"Yes, mother, I bring home twelve thousand dollars."

Mrs. Carr could not believe it at first, but Herbert told his story, and she gave joyful credence at last.

Eben did not receive as warm a welcome, but finally his father was propitiated, and agreed to give his son employment in his own store. He's there yet. His hard experience in the West has subdued his pride, and he has really "turned over a new leaf," as he promised Herbert. His father will probably next year give him a quarter interest in the firm, and the firm's name will be

"EBENEZER GRAHAM & SON."

Herbert and his mother have moved to Boston. Our hero is learning business in the counting room of Mr. Compton. They live in a pleasant house at the South End, and Mr. Melville, restored to a very fair measure of health, is boarding, or, rather, has his home with them. He is devoting his time to literary pursuits, and I am told that he is the author of a brilliant paper in a recent number of the North American Review. Herbert finds some time for study, and, under the guidance of his friend and former employer, he has already become a very creditable scholar in French, German and English literature. He enjoys his present prosperity all the better for the hardships through which he passed before reaching it.

THE END

www.ingramcontent.com/pod-product-compliance
Lightning Source LLC
Chambersburg PA
CBHW081724100526
44591CB00016B/2492

www.ingramcontent.com/pod-product-compliance
Lightning Source LLC
Chambersburg PA
CBHW081724100526
44591CB00016B/2492